Good Eats J

A Local's Guide to the Best Independently-Owned Restaurants Along Florida's First Coast

Andrew Paul Williams

with

Lois Virginia Strickland Williams

Copyright 2019

Williams Press LLC

All Rights Reserved

ISBN: 978-0-9979610-1-0

About Mom

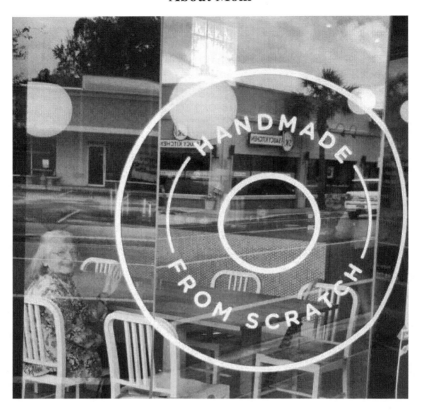

Virginia Williams is graduate of Georgia College for Women and a retired Elementary School Teacher who also taught High School classes in Chemistry and Home Economics in her early career. Originally from Brian County, Georgia (near Savannah), she has lived in the Jacksonville, Florida area for many decades and enjoys frequenting local restaurants.

About Andrew

Andrew Paul Williams, Ph.D. (Mass Communication, University of Florida) is an author, public speaker and consultant who approaches his work from international and interdisciplinary perspectives. He earned his M.A. in English and B.A. in Communications and English from the University of North Florida. He is also received his 200 and 300 hour Yoga Teacher Certification from Yoga Den and is registered as an RYT 500 with Yoga Alliance. He works as a communications practitioner, working as Public Relations and Social Media Manager for Grady H. Williams, Jr. LL.M. Attorneys at Law, P.A. and as a Yoga Instructor for Yoga Den at their Mandarin, Fleming Island, and World Golf Village Studios. He taught communications classes at Virginia Tech, University of Florida, and Flagler College. He has also worked as a writer for *Where, Jacksonville Magazine, Financial News & Daily Record*, and *The Clay County Leader*. He has written about food professionally since the early 90s and is an enthusiastic supporter and promoter of the local food scene in his home town of Jacksonville, Florida.

Foreword

By Judy Wells

I have watched Andrew Williams grow up since I was in college and he was a precocious squirt working at the local weekly. We lived in Orange Park, which then was a quick stop on the daily Greyhound route and no one else's. In that small locale, the height of our culinary experiences beyond our mother's fare ranged from a pseudo Chinese/Polynesian restaurant to a burger at the local drugstore counter.

Over the years as we traveled away from home and into the world our taste buds received a thorough education. A "good" meal took on a new, more exacting definition. Whether grabbing street food or dining in Michelin-starred restaurants, we learned to appreciate the food as well as its settings.

We kept challenging our taste buds with new flavors and experiencing worlds far beyond our tiny town adolescence, during which if anyone wanted a gourmet meal in Jacksonville, we sent them to St. Augustine.

Our paths crossed between travels, mostly in Jacksonville's lively arts community, but we lived in separate worlds, Andrew in modeling and post-graduate education, me in journalism.

By the new millennium, we were back on the First Coast and began having lunch together, introducing one another to new restaurants in different parts of town. Now we could stay in Jacksonville for a good, even fine, meal, be it Thai, Italian, hip Asian, Indian, French, German, Fusion, seafood or Southern.

Every week another one or two new spots would pop up. Andrew kept saying the city needed a book about its culinary explosion. I agreed, and we talked about what form it should take. Andrew's mother, Virginia, began joining us and her comments were so perfect we decided Mom needed to be in there, too.

Most such projects would have died with table talk, but Andrew bit into the idea and persisted. I am so proud of him and honored to have been a very small part of this book's birthing.

I hope you enjoy using it to explore the area's ever-growing food scene, finding renewed pleasure in old stand-bys and excitement and satisfaction in the plethora of new options.

As you do, count on Andrew, Mom and me to keep looking for more temptations.

A 20-year veteran of The Florida Times-Union, Judy Wells has written on travel and food for publications such as The Washington Post, The Philadelphia Inquirer, Boston Globe, Palm Beach Post and AAA magazines. She can be heard talking travel with Melissa Ross on Community Connect, WJCT-FM. A member of the Society of American Travel Writers and the Women's Food Alliance, she produces travel content for Global Traveler and All Things Cruise as well as her own sites, WellsWorld.net, Travel on the Level and Food Afar.

Contents

Introduction

I began this book a few years ago thinking that I really knew the local food scene, and I was wrong.

From food trucks to fine dining with white linen table cloths there is a lot more going on in the Jacksonville area than I would have ever imagined, and I've been active in seeking out cool local places to eat for decades.

The food was incredible, but the people made this project, and I'm grateful mom was willing and able to help me with this book. Including mom was practical and enjoyable. She was recovering from a fall and a head injury and getting out a lot did her wonders. A defining moment in her recovery was when she perked up while sitting outside at Taverna when she ordered a Cobb salad telling me enthusiastically how much she enjoyed it and eating there.

We did an exhaustive search from local publications, Trip Advisor, Yelp, following local social media gurus, Google, word of mouth, driving around, and great tips from friends and the nice people we've met along the way.

This book kept growing on us. One restaurant would lead to four others. The obvious and hidden treasures that we'd been by many times, revisiting places from childhood, and discovering new places gave us a lot of fun drives, meals, and good conversations with new friends.

My late father, Reverend Grady H. Williams, Sr., loved several of these places and would drive us all over when I was a child not thinking anything of waiting in a parking lot for over an hour for a good shrimp dinner. We've thought and talked about him a lot during this work and know how he and other family and friends we miss would enjoy what we're doing. There have been lots of wonderful times with friends and family during the work

Each restaurant can seem like its own world, and the time in these environments helped me see and appreciate northeast Florida in new ways. We've loved this culinary expedition of Florida's First Coast and surrounding areas. Jacksonville is the largest city land wise in the continental United States, and we did our best to cover as much of it as we could the last few years going to both obscure and obvious eateries to include in this publication.

If we missed one of your favorites, please let me know so I can include it in the next addition. We plan to update Good Eats Jax annually. (If you'd like, you can visit our website at goodeatsjax.com or email me at andrew@williamspress.com.)

We hope you enjoy trying these wonderful places as much as we have.

All the best,
Andrew and Virginia

Downtown Jacksonville

Like many cities, our downtown has gone through several transformations in my lifetime. What used to be large departments stores are now large office buildings and local government offices, and shopping is rather limited. However, a number of brilliant and innovative business owners and creatives keep adding to our city's urban offerings, and with the MOCA downtown, art walks, a popular football team, and a number of outstanding restaurants, downtown Jacksonville is something to be proud of.

Bellwether

100 N Laura St #100, Jacksonville, FL 32202

(904) 802-7745 https://bellwetherjax.com/

(Mom loves going downtown to eat at Bellwether!)

Why we like it: An incredible dining experience in a cool urban space with a nice bar, bar dining area, and dining room. Fantastic service, outstanding food, and a real city feel, Bellwether is a great downtown Jacksonville destination. They also have complimentary valet parking.

What we enjoy here: We enjoy the Pimento and Cheese and Boiled Peanuts. Mom loves the deconstructed Chicken and Dumplings, and I love their fresh catch in the light broth. We recently took our good friends who were in town from Atlanta and had a fantastic experience. A definite favorite with a modern, city feel.

Mom says: Now *this* is *really* fine dining in a big city!

(When our good friends from Atlanta, Patrick and Cindy Flynn, came to visit us recently we were proud to take them to Downtown Jacksonville to Bellwether.)

Café Nola at MOCA

333 N Laura St, Jacksonville, FL 32202

(904) 224-0113 http://www.mocajax.org/cafe/

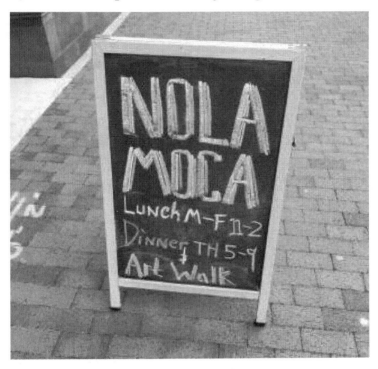

Why we like it: An incredible dining experience in our city's more modern museum.

What we enjoy here: The hot rolls are always a treat, and I love their steak or seafood special. Mom loves their sandwiches and salads. It is always good, and the service is professional. Desserts vary, and they are always worth it. Good wine, beer, and tea here too.

Mom says: You almost feel like you're in a movie when you come here. I really like it!

Chamblin's Bookmine Uptown Cafe

215 N Laura St, Jacksonville, FL 32202

(904) 674-0868 www.chamblinbookmine.com/default.aspx

Why we like it: We love Chamblin's and having a light meal or an afternoon dessert in a favorite bookstore's downtown location is something we both find so pleasant. There's always an interesting mix of people.

What we enjoy: Soups, sandwiches, cupcakes, and cookies. A nice hot cup of tea or coffee. We recently shared a lemon square. It was homemade and delicious tasting.

Mom says: I love a nice treat here. Such a great thing to have downtown and the people who work here make you feel welcome.

Cowford Chophouse

101 E Bay St, Jacksonville, FL 32202

(904) 862-6464 http://cowfordchophouse.com/

Why we like it: Upscale and an impressive city steakhouse with a large bar and dining area on the ground floor, a second floor for formal dining, and a scenic rooftop lounge.

What we enjoy here: We took a friend for her birthday and went all out. We shared the Christmas Bacon for an appetizer, Mom had Risotto, Stephanie had a Filet, and I had a Ribeye. We shared some nice sides of potatoes and asparagus, and a delicious classic dessert. Everything was first class with excellent service.

Mom says: This place is really nice and definitely a treat to eat here.

Happy Grilled Cheese

219 N Hogan St, Jacksonville, FL 32202

(904) 423-0318

http://thehappygrilledchees.wixsite.com/grilledcheese

Why we like it: Awesome casual downtown spot. This food-truck-turned-restaurant is an incredible treat.

What we enjoy here: Mom had one with bacon and tomato, and I had one with barbeque and macaroni and cheese. Rich, delicious, and great fresh fries too!

Mom says: this grilled cheese sandwich is so rich. I can't believe I'm eating this much. So good!

Indochine

21 E Adams St #200, Jacksonville, FL 32202

(904) 598-5303 http://www.indochinejax.com/

Why we like it: Beautiful Thai restaurant downtown that has food that is up to par with the décor.

What we enjoy here: Mom loves their Pad Thai, I love the Drunken noodles, and the crab Rangoon, and steamed dumplings, which are all top notch here, as are their soups, salads, and desserts. Top rate versions of Thai favorites abound on the menu.

(Excellent Pad Thai at Indochine Downtown Jacksonville)

Mom says: I love these noodles!

Olio Restaurant

301 E Bay St, Jacksonville, FL 32202

(904) 356-7100 http://www.oliomarket.com/

Why we like it: One of the most beautiful and urban cool spaces I've been to in any area. I love the food, people, bright sunny corner it's on, and just loved being here. Mom was like a kid in a candy store.

What we enjoy here: Mom had their famous Duck Grilled Cheese, and I had Shrimp Tacos. We shared a piece of the Butterscotch Carrot Cake with Buttercream Icing. Everything was incredible.

Mom says: I am enjoying sitting here downtown and love how bright and open it is.

(Mom was thrilled with Olio and this sandwich!)

Springfield

Beautiful historic Springfield is one of our favorite places to visit because my mom, dad and other family once lived there; and also, its distinct cool feel. There are a number of options here that I have made the trip for regularly and highly suggest you do too.

Crispy's Springfield Gallery

1735 Main St N, Jacksonville, FL 32206

(904) 661-1503 http://www.crispysspringfieldgallery.com/

Why we like it: It's a cool urban old building that is fun to spend time in. Nice people and good food.

What we enjoy here: We loved the pizza and our server let us make it a combination of two types.

Mom says: It's wonderful having a good meal in Springfield.

Uptown Kitchen and Bar

1303 Main St N, Jacksonville, FL 32206

(904) 355-0734 https://uptownkitchenjax.com/

Why we like it: This is a top-notch place in Springfield that offers consistently good breakfast, lunch, and dinner.

What we enjoy here: We enjoy their fish and grits, salads, sandwiches, and desserts.

Mom says: What a beautiful place with such good food and service!

(Coffee and Pecan Pie at Uptown Kitchen: awesome!)

San Marco

San Marco remains a favorite historic neighborhood for local shopping and dining.

BB's Restaurant and Bar

1019 Hendricks Ave, Jacksonville, FL 32207

(904) 306-0100 https://bbsrestaurant.com/

Why we like it: A favorite place for brunch, lunch, dinner or dessert. You can't miss here. Everything is good. It's consistent. Nice upscale environment with a cool bar and decadent deserts on display.

(A fun Saturday Brunch at BB's with Mom and John Meeks—one of her favorite students who is now also an educator.)

What we enjoy here: Don't skip dessert. The dessert case is legendary here. My favorite is the Oreo Mouse Cake. The Chocolate Cake is insane. Crab Cakes, Fresh Catch, Chicken and Waffles, Steak, Caesar Salad--You name it, it's good here. Excellent service, good parking, and nice environment.

Mom says: It is always a special treat coming to such a beautiful place!

(Mom and BB's owner Barbara Bredehoeft in front of the desserts. Mom says she feels like a celebrity meeting all these people!)

The Bearded Pig

1224 Kings Ave, Jacksonville, FL 32207

(904) 619-2247 http://thebeardedpigbbq.com/

Why we like it: This is a super cool urban feeling place. Chad Munsey has done an awesome job with the environment, food, and service.

What we enjoy here: We enjoy sitting in the back-yard area and having a sampler of meats, macaroni and cheese, coleslaw and delicious sides. The Banana pudding is great here too, and they have a nice bar and dining area inside. Plus, they have outdoor space for families and children to enjoy.

Mom says: It so good and nice seeing everyone having a fun time.

Bistro Aix

1440 San Marco Blvd, Jacksonville, FL 32207

(904) 398-1949 http://www.bistrox.com/

Why we like it: A favorite Jacksonville French bistro that is still as beautiful and delicious as ever.

What we enjoy here: They have wonderful soups, salads, pizzas, fish, steak *frites*, lobster crepes, and outstanding pastries.

Mom says: I love this super crispy thin pizza. Too good!

(Bistro Aix offers beautiful indoor, outdoor and lounge areas.)

Good Dough

1636 Hendricks Ave, Jacksonville, FL 32207

(904) 527-1875 https://www.gooddoughdoughnuts.com/

Why we like it: Very hip gourmet donut place that offers an excellent assortment to choose from.

What we enjoy here: It's a lot of modern twists and taking things you love to the next level. The grilled cheese and tomato soup is so comforting, the fried chicken donut is decadent, and the donuts are beyond expectations. So good!

Mom says: This is good stuff!

(Maple Glazed and a Chocolate Glazed with Chocolate and Sea Salt Caramel at Good Dough.)

Matthew's Restaurant

2107 Hendricks Ave, Jacksonville, FL 32207

(904) 396-9922 http://matthewsrestaurant.com/

Why we like it: Great for a special occasion. Beautiful upscale restaurant that's been a Jacksonville treasure since the late 90s.

What we like here: Everything is spectacular. Mom loves the airline chicken. I love a steak here or seafood. Make sure to order a souffle when you order your entrée.

Mom says: This is a place to come and celebrate!

(Matthew's knows how to make you feel like a VIP guest.)

Peterbrooke Chocolatier

2024 San Marco Blvd, Jacksonville, FL 32207

(904) 398-2488 https://www.peterbrooke.com/

Why we like it: A Jacksonville favorite chocolate shop that will never let you down. Plus, they have excellent ice cream!

What we enjoy here: Mom loves the white chocolate ice cream and the marshmallows dipped in chocolate. I love the cookies and cream ice cream and the chocolate covered popcorn.

Mom says: This is a nice place you can always count on to find something good.

Rue St Mark

2103 San Marco Blvd, Jacksonville, FL 32207

(904) 619-0861 https://ruesaintmarc.com/

Why we like it: So French and a beautiful space. Professional and knowledgeable service.

What we enjoy here: We've enjoyed their assorted Farmstead Cheese Selection, the Pork and Foie Gras Pâté, and Eggplant Beignets. Mom loves the quiche, and I like their Fish Meunière. Their Lemon Tart and Chocolate Crème Brulee are excellent.

Mom says: Definitely a special experience.

(Absolutely perfect cheese board and pate at Rue. St. Mark—one of our favorite new additions to the San Marco area and Jacksonville food scene.)

Taverna

1986 San Marco Blvd, Jacksonville, FL 32207

(904) 398-3005 http://www.taverna.restaurant/

Why we like it: A top favorite for superior Italian cuisine.

What we enjoy here: Mom loves the roast chicken. I love the ribeye special. Olives, house made pasta, pizza, meatballs, shrimp. You name it, it's all great here. Have dessert. The gelato and sorbettos are superb, as are their cookies and seasonal offerings.

(Mom opted for the Smoked Chicken dinner special recently at Taverna, and she was justifiably impressed.)

Mom says: Taverna is one of my favorite places, and it is always a great time! I like sitting outside here too. The people know how to treat you nicely.

The Wine Cellar

1314 Prudential Dr, Jacksonville, FL 32207

(904) 398-8989 http://www.winecellarjax.com/index.html

Why we like it: A Jacksonville landmark that is still outstanding for lunch and dinner.

What we enjoy here: I love their fish specials and always a fan of their Salmon. Mom loves their pastas. Desserts are excellent classics. Great service and old-world atmosphere. You can dine outside if the weather permits, and it's a wonderful experience.

Mom says: This reminds me of my grandparents and aunts and uncles and their big old houses. Beautiful place and delicious food.

(Mom and I enjoying the Wine Cellar with our good friend, Judy Wells.)

Town Hall

2012 San Marco Blvd, Jacksonville, FL 32207

(904) 398-0726 https://www.townhalljax.com/

Why we like it: Modern hip cool offering by brilliant chef Tom Gray.

What we enjoy here: Mom loved the pasta, and I had an incredible lamb entrée.

Mom says: There's a lot going on here. I like it!

The Write Touch

1967 San Marco Blvd, Jacksonville, FL 32207

(904) 398-2009   https://thewritetouch.com/

Why we like it: This beautiful stationary and gift shop is a Jacksonville institution, and each holiday season they bring back a tradition started by its original owner, the legendary Doris Mellion: decadent chocolate covered buttery toffee made by the nuns at Mount Saint Mary's Abbey. I typically order two boxes a year, and love going to this wonderful place to pick them up.

What we enjoy here: The Trappistine Milk Chocolate Butter Nut Munch is a special indulgence we look forward to each Christmas.

Mom says: This is a rich and delicious chocolate treat.

San Jose / Lakewood

A wonderful older Jacksonville area that has a few fantastic places for breakfast, lunch, and dinner.

The Book Nook

1620 University Blvd W, Jacksonville, FL 32217

(904) 733-4586

Why we like it: We are very fond of this local bookstore and gift shop because of the people and all the great things we've found here over the years, but especially because they carry one of the most iconic, Old Jacksonville confections imaginable: Annaclaire Chocolates.

What we enjoy here: These sweet vanilla creams, rolled in pecans, and dipped in milk or dark chocolate were a favorite that recall trips to the old May Cohen's Department Store.

Mom says: It so special getting to come here and get a box of these chocolates. It takes me back to many happy times.

Carroll's Meat Shoppe Seafood & Produce Market

6861 St Augustine Rd, Jacksonville, FL 32217

(904) 268-1535

Why we like it: A charming southern grocery with excellent meats and produce. Small and friendly place that's been an Old San Jose standby for decades.

What we enjoy here: Steaks, Ribs, local honey, nice fruits and vegetables. It's like going back in time—in a good way.

Mom says: This is so nice and old fashioned. Love these Georgia Peaches and the fresh produce.

Comfort. A Southern Bistro

2777 University Blvd W #32, Jacksonville, FL 32217

(904) 683-7182

Why we like it: We found out about his place because of our cousin Troy, and like her and her husband Keith, we think this is a great spot in Lakewood for excellent country cooking.

What we enjoy here: We loved the fried appetizers of Green Tomatoes, Okra, and Green Beans, the Deviled Eggs, and the Pimento Bruschetta. Mom thought the Fried Chicken was very good, and I liked their Shrimp and Grits.

Mom says: This is a neat place that definitely has good comfort food.

(Mom and her first cousin, Troy, who introduced us to this great place and treated us to a wonderful Sunday Brunch.)

Famous Amos

3911 University Blvd W, Jacksonville, FL 32207

(904) 731-2322

Why we like it: The quintessential "greasy spoon" this is a great diner and country cooking favorite for many locals, and you can't go wrong there for breakfast, lunch, dinner, and late-night meals. They don't have as many locations as they used to, but they still have another in Mandarin and on the West Side.

What we enjoy here: The breakfast foods are great. Terrific biscuits and cornbread. Country vegetable plates, fried chicken, chicken livers, chicken and dumplings, turkey and dressing, roast beef. You can't go wrong here with the classics. Great cobblers and ice box pies.

Mom says: MMM. So country. Delicious!

The French Pantry

6301 Powers Ave, Jacksonville, FL 32217

(904) 730-8696 https://thefrenchpantry.com/

Why we like it: It's just so amazing on all levels and well worth the drive to an industrial area of town and a wait in line.

What we like here: Lunch here is a fantastic experience. Strawberry wedding cake. Chicken salad. Bread basket with olive oil. Traditional real food. I recently had a poached salmon eggs benedict here that was almost an otherworldly experience.

Mom says: "Remember the name of this place and make a note to take me back here soon."

Sorrento

6943 St Augustine Rd, Jacksonville, FL 32217

(904) 636-9196

Why we like it: An old-fashioned Jacksonville standby for classic Italian food in a cozy setting with good service.

What we enjoy here: Pasta for mom. Seafood special for me. They were classic and so delicious, as were the bread and salad.

Mom says: This takes me back. We need to come here more often.

(Mom loved the Tortellini Alfredo and bread at Sorrento.)

The Local

4578 San Jose Blvd, Jacksonville, FL 32207

(904) 683-8063   https://www.thelocaljax.com/

Why we like it: Cool urban feeling coffee shop, bar, café.

What we enjoy here: Mom had a huge fried chicken and waffle plate that included scrambled eggs and bacon. I had steak and eggs. I had a huge fresh and delicious salad with grilled chicken. Outstanding!

(Mom was really impressed with her brunch at The Local.)

Mom says: I can never eat this much, but it is fantastic!

Pepe's Hacienda & Restaurant

3615 Dupont Ave # 900, Jacksonville, FL 32217

(904) 636-8131

Why we like it: Authentic Mexican restaurant and grocery store with nice people and excellent food.

What we enjoy here: I love the tamales, mom loves the enchilada and chili relleno. Excellent house made chips too.

(Mom gives Pepe's an enthusiastic thumbs up, as do I.)

Mom says: What a great experience coming here!

Toscana Little Italy

4440 Hendricks Ave, Jacksonville, FL 32207

(904) 900-1059   http://www.toscanajax.com/

Why we like it: Impressive traditional Italian neighborhood spot.

What we enjoy here: All the classics. Excellent bread, shrimp appetizer, mom's favorite tortellini, fresh catch Francaise is top notch. Excellent chocolate bomb for dessert.

Mom says: this place is really special. Excellent service too.

The Yum Yum Tree

6225 St Augustine Rd, Jacksonville, FL 32217

(904) 731-0957

Why we like it: Old school tea room vibe and southern café happening big time.

What we enjoy here: Fantastic chicken salad, crepes, quiche, and sandwiches. Love the cheese and cracker, fruit or tossed salad. Great pies and ice-cream crepes. We LOVE this place forever now and miss the ones in Avondale and Orange Park.

Mom says: I'm so glad they are still here. Definitely a favorite!

(Hello from a long-time favorite place. We are always happy for lunch at The Yum Yum Tree!)

Riverside

Beautiful historic Riverside has always been a cool place to enjoy a good meal, and the revitalization of Five Points and King Street areas make it even more so. There are many outstanding options in this area.

Black Sheep Restaurant

1534 Oak St, Jacksonville, FL 32204

(904) 380-3091   https://blacksheep5points.com/

(Celebrating Mother's Day at a favorite place: Blacksheep!)

Why we like it: Modern, innovative, and classic, this beautiful restaurant has incredible indoor, outdoor, bar, and rooftop seating in historic Five Points. Excellent everything. Managing Partner, Allan DeVault and his entire team do an excellent job making this a premier destination and a world-class dining experience.

What we enjoy here: Chicken liver pate, fried olives, steak, chicken, sustainable fresh catch, Sunday fried chicken dinner, brunch, lunch, desserts, always special. They have craft cocktails, beers, and an extensive wine list.

(The Family Style Sunday Night Fried Chicken Dinner at Black Sheep is a winner, as is everything they do here.)

(The sustainable fresh catch is so amazing and one of the reasons Black Sheep is one of my favorite restaurants in Jacksonville.)

Mom says: This another really neat big city type of place that's so good with people who make it a special experience.

Bold Bean Coffee Roasters

869 Stockton St, Jacksonville, FL 32204

(904) 853-6545   https://www.boldbeancoffee.com/

Why we like it: Bustling urban feeling coffee shop with outstanding sweet baked goods, savory treats, coffee and teas. Nice, interesting people.

What we enjoy here: mom likes a piece of quiche and a cookie. I love a pour-over and the flourless chocolate cookie.

Mom says: I feel like I'm a part of what's going on with the younger folks when we come here.

(Mom and me with our dear friend, Melissa after at Bold Bean Yoga last November. Melissa passed away after a short illness this May, just a few months after this photo was taken. She was enthusiastic about, and supportive of, this project. It is bittersweet finishing this now and not being able to celebrate with her. But she's in our hearts as we enjoy the best of local Jacksonville, which she loved.)

Bread and Board

1030 Oak St, Jacksonville, FL 32204

(904) 862-6992   http://thebreadandboard.com/

Why we like it: An excellent lunch spot in a repurposed Five Points building and front yard space.

What we enjoy here: Huge burgers and cake.

Mom says: Enough to share and to take some home. Very good!

(We enjoyed our lunch at Bread and Board and especially loved the use of outdoor space in this beautiful part of historic Five Points.)

BREW Five Points

1024 Park St, Jacksonville, FL 32204

(904) 374-5789   http://brewfivepoints.com/

Why we like it: A definite favorite place, this super cool coffee shop, bakery, café, and wine / craft beer haven is like a trip to New York.

What we enjoy here: With its superstar baker, Callie Marie (author of Callie Marie Bakes) you can have some of the best cake, pastry and sweet and savory kolaches found anywhere. They also have wonderful salads, avocado toast and other daily specials.

Mom says: I remember going to Goode's Bakery across the street many years ago. It's nice having this wonderful place to enjoy now.

(Mom loving BREW Five Points.)

Cool Moose Café

2708 Park St, Jacksonville, FL 32205

(904) 381-4242   http://www.coolmoosecafe.net/

Why we like it: It is always a relaxed and enjoyable time visiting this neighborhood spot in Riverside. They live up to their mission of "Serving delicious affordable food and an expansive selection of coffee all while making you a part of our family."

What we enjoy here: For their breakfast items, I am a fan of the omelets and meat lover's plate. Mom loves their muffins. Their ham and brie sandwich and avocado sandwich are real winners for lunch. Everything is fresh, delicious, and served by friendly people who make you feel at home.

Mom says: You always see someone nice here, and the food is just wholesome and delicious.

Corner Taco

818 Post St, Jacksonville, FL 32204

(904) 240-0412   https://www.cornertaco.com/

Why we like it: A favorite spot for gourmet Mexican street style food.

What we enjoy here: yuca fries, fried chicken and shrimp tacos, tenderloin and cherry tacos, fish tacos. They do the tacos in corn, flour or lettuce wraps. Mexican Coke and beer, wine or tea complete a good meal, as do the chips and salsa.

Mom says: I want to go back here and soon!

(Fried Shrimp and Fried Chicken Tacos and a Mexican Coke: Mom's in her happy place at Corner Taco.)

Crane Ramen

1029 Park St, Jacksonville, FL 32204

(904) 253-3282   https://www.craneramen904.com/

Why we like it: Hip and cool Asian offering in Five Points. Nice outdoor and indoor dining and a bar area.

What we enjoy here: The small Ramen bowls are great. We also enjoyed sharing a Fried Chicken Bites appetizer.

Mom says: This is the small size? Too much good food!

The Cummer Museum Café

829 Riverside Ave, Jacksonville, FL 32204

(904) 899-6022   https://www.cummermuseum.org/visit/cafe

Why we like it: Wonderful spot for brunch, lunch, or tapas

What we enjoy here: I love the blue cheese potato chips and crab cakes Benedict, and mom loves their quiche and sandwiches.

Mom says: It is always a treat having this delicious food at the museum.

(Incredible Kale and Grilled Shrimp Salad at Cummer Café.)

Foo Dog Curry Traders

869 Stockton St, Jacksonville, FL 32204

(904) 551-0327   http://foodogjax.com/

Why we like it: Street food vibe for sure and a cool urban feel for Jacksonville.

What we enjoy here: Zucchini Fritters, Wild Ginger and Mushroom Noodles, and Crispy cod with green curry are outstanding. I don't think you can go wrong here with anything.

Mom says: What city is this? I feel like I'm in New York.

Grassroots Natural Market

2007 Park St, Jacksonville, FL 32204

(904) 384-4474   http://www.thegrassrootsmarket.com/

Why we like it: I love shopping here, getting premade things, great produce, grass-fed beef, farm eggs, smoothies and juices, and nice deli options for a meal on the go. Excellent resource for vegan and paleo diets. Great frozen food and organic options. Good selection of soups, pasta sauces, and bone broth.

What we enjoy here: Daily Detox is one of my favorites. The cheese selection is first rate.

Mom says: beautiful selection of fruits and vegetables.

Hovan Gourmet Mediterranean

2005 Park St, Jacksonville, FL 32204

(904) 381-9394   http://www.hovan5points.com/

Why we like it: Outstanding Greek food, love sitting outside.

What we enjoy here: Hummus with warm pita bread, lamb, chicken. Baklava!

(We loved sitting outside enjoying Five Points and the delicious dinner at Hovan.)

Mom says: I had a great time here!

Lola's Burrito Joint

1522 King St, Jacksonville, FL 32205

(904) 738-7181   http://lolasburritojoint.com/

Why we like it: Casual and consistently good neighborhood spot in Riverside with cool décor and vibe.

What we enjoy here: Mom and I love the Yucky Yuca Fries. I am a big fan of their shrimp and fish tacos, and Mom likes the cheeseburger and the chicken burrito.

Mom says: It's fun being in this neighborhood at such a fun place.

Mossfire Grill

1537 Margaret St, Jacksonville, FL 32204

(904) 355-4434   http://www.mossfire.com/

Why we like it: Excellent southwestern food and service in a comfortable Five Points mainstay.

What we enjoy here: I love their fish specials and mom loves the chicken. Everything is fantastic.

Mom says: Flavorful and seems pretty healthy too.

(Excellent Crab Cake Salad at Mossfire)

Nacho Taco

751 Stockton St, Jacksonville, FL 32204

(904) 619-0383

Why we like it: Very good tiny spot that has excellent tacos.

What we enjoy here: Outstanding yuca fries, chips, salsa, and soft-shell tacos.

Mom says: A taco in the car or at one of the picnic tables is good for me!

Primi Piata

2722 Park St, Jacksonville, FL 32205

(904) 389-5545

Why we like it: classic refined and relaxed Italian restaurant.

What we enjoy here: some of the best pasta and tortellini and outstanding fresh seafood specials. Homemade tiramisu.

Mom says: very nice and high quality.

rain dogs.

3907, 1045 Park St, Jacksonville, FL 32204

(904) 379-4969

Why we like it: Such a cool bar, art gallery, and performance space that is to me the true heart of Five Points. Christina Wagner is a hero!

What we enjoy here: This is a fun place to get a beer or wine, see a band, hang with friends, dance some, and enjoy delicious hummus, grilled cheese, nachos, and other far-from-average bar food. I've had excellent olives, boiled peanuts, and other perfect snacks to go with a good glass of red wine numerous times here. Everything is very good, the people are nice, and it's a true indie experience.

Mom says: I haven't been invited here yet. This might be one for the younger folks!

Bakery Ribault

3901, 813 Lomax St, Jacksonville, FL 32204

(904) 683-5074   https://bakeryribault.com/

Why we like it: Outstanding upscale bakery in Five Points.

What we enjoy here: Pain au chocolat, cakes, pastries. Everything.

Mom says: Now this is good!

(Decadent treats at Bakery Ribault.)

River and Post

1000 Riverside Ave #100, Jacksonville, FL 32204

(904) 575-2366   https://www.riverandpostjax.com/

Why we like it: A lively upscale seafood restaurant with a real city feel. Bustling dining room and rooftop seating.

What we enjoy here: Mom likes the crab cakes. I enjoy the fresh catch.

Mom says: Definitely makes you feel like you are like in a big city.

(Another fun research dinner with Judy Wells at River & Post.)

Sake House

824 Lomax St, Jacksonville, FL 32204

(904) 301-1188   http://www.sakehousejax.com/

Why we like it: Consistently good Japanese fare.

What we enjoy here: Mom likes the Chicken Katsu or stir fry and I love their sushi and edamame.

Mom says: Great flavor and great service.

(Fun Sushi Presentation at Sake House)

Southern Roots

1275 King St, Jacksonville, FL 32204

(904) 513-4726   https://www.southernrootsjax.com/

Why we like it: Casual delicious vegetarian food.

What we enjoy here: Excellent salads, greens and rice bowls, and baked goods.

Mom says: I enjoy the sweet treats here a lot.

The Stuffed Beaver

2548 Oak St, Jacksonville, FL 32204

(904) 240-1980

Why we like it: Fun Canadian-themed casual spot for lunch.

What we enjoy here: Mom loves the crepes and I'm a fan of their poutine.

(The Ham and Cheese Crepe at The Stuffed Beaver was a real winner.)

Mom says: I can't believe how good this is and the huge servings.

Sweet Theory Baking Co.

1243 King St, Jacksonville, FL 32204

(904) 387-1001

(One of the most charming and delicious places in Jacksonville: Sweet Theory.)

Why we like it: Old school bakery feel here with awesome gluten free and classic offerings.

What we enjoy here: Coffee cake, chocolate donut, and whatever catches our eye. Everything is beyond incredible. Great cinnamon rolls.

Mom says: Old timey and outstanding baked goods!

13 Gypsies

887 Stockton St, Jacksonville, FL 32204

(904) 389-0330   http://www.13gypsies.com/

Why we like it: Chef driven small outstanding place.

What we enjoy here: Their gnocchi is beyond anything I've ever had. Great seafood and tapas. Everything is first rate.

Mom says: Such a nice place!

Two Dudes Seafood

2665 Park St, Jacksonville, FL 32204

(904) 337-1699   http://www.twodudesrestaurant.com/

Why we like it: This outstanding Atlantic Beach mainstay also recently opened in Riverside, on the corner of King and Park Streets, and it is a much-needed new seafood spot in town.

What we enjoy here: We love the Crab Cakes and the Grilled Scallops at Two Dudes. Fresh and delicious. Some of the best of both you'll find. Go all out and try the fried loaded potato or Wasabi Slaw, if you're feeling adventurous.

(A memorable late Sunday lunch at Two Dudes. Mom was reasonably thrilled with this experience, the excellent food, and personable service.)

Mom says: There's no filler in this crab cake. Delicious!

Avondale

The beautiful historic Avondale neighborhood is home to some of the very best dining around, and I have many good childhood memories from being with my family and friends here.

Old Cup Cafe

3604 St Johns Ave, Jacksonville, FL 32205

(904) 389-2122 https://odcup.business.site/

(Mom having a blast visiting Old Cup Cafe)

Why we like it: Charming coffee and sweet shop located in historic Avondale. Nice assortment of cupcakes, cookies, and other baked goods.

What we enjoy here: Mom had the Red Velvet Cupcake and I tried the German Chocolate. Both were great.

Mom says: Mmm hmm wonderful!

Barrique Kitchen and Wine Bar

3563 St Johns Ave, Jacksonville, FL 32205

(904) 619-2150   https://www.barriqueofavondale.com/

Why we like it: Upscale, accommodating, and comfortable with excellent small plates, desserts, and extensive wine list serving brunch, lunch, and dinner. Their focus is on sociable sharing. From tuna tartare to braised short ribs to Spanish style octopus to creole shrimp and grits, this eclectic eatery is a welcome addition to the historic Avondale neighborhood.

What we enjoy here: I've only been for lunch and had an incredible duck special.

Mom says: When are you taking me? I'm ready!

Biscottis

3556 St Johns Ave, Jacksonville, FL 32205

(904) 387-2060   http://biscottis.net/

(One of many great family celebrations with mom and my brother, Grady H. Williams, Jr., at Biscotti's)

Why we like it: This has been one of our favorite places for 25 years. When the first opened it was very small with excellent coffee and muffins, and it's evolved into one of the best fine dining/casual cafés around.

What we enjoy here: Everything is very good. The pizzas, sandwiches, awesome Salmon Salad, Bruschetta, Steak, Seafood Specials, Pork Chop. Don't skip dessert. It's always worth it, and they are big enough to share.

Mom says: Biscotti's is so lively and has consistently good eats.

Blue Fish

3551 St Johns Ave, Jacksonville, FL 32205

(904) 387-0700   https://bluefishjax.com/

Why we like it: Consistently good and fresh. Love the back courtyard.

What we enjoy here: Mom likes the shrimp and crab cakes and I typically go for the fresh catch. Very good food, and excellent service. Great salads and desserts too.

Mom says: It's relaxing sitting out back by the fountain here. Nice place.

Chomp Chomp

4162 Herschel St, Jacksonville, FL 32210

(904) 329-1679

(Having a fun and delicious lunch at Chomp Chomp with Judy Wells)

Why we like it: Another incredible place from our friend, Ian Chase. Casual and excellent food in old Fairfax area between Avondale and Ortega. Great outdoor place with a few booths and counter inside.

What we enjoy here: Everything is really good at Chomp Chomp. We love the burgers, the Bahn Mi, the daily specials are excellent as are the desserts. Excellent salads and Chicken Satay too. Incredible Curry Potato Chips!

Mom says: Such a nice easy-going place with friendly people and great food.

(Mom loves Chomp Chomp!)

J. William Culinary

4260 Herschel St, Jacksonville, FL 32210

(904) 516-7098   https://www.jwilliamculinary.com/

Why we like it: Chef-driven and healthy meals and treats to go. This guy is Internationally known for paleo food for good reason. Awesome place. They also offer a delivery service.

What we enjoy here: Everything is delicious. Chicken, pork, meatballs, wings, ribs, sweet potatoes. You can boil in a bag or heat in the oven the ready-made meals. Great combination of flavors.

Mom says: This is my kind of food!

MOJO no.4, Urban BBQ Whiskey Bar

3572 St Johns Ave, Jacksonville, FL 32205

(904) 381-6670   https://mojobbq.com/

Why we like it: all of these local mojos are good.

What we enjoy here: Beef and pork especially. Great sides. Love the burnt ends.

Mom says: Hearty servings and flavorful barbeque.

Restaurant Orsay

3630 Park St, Jacksonville, FL 32205

(904) 381-0909   http://www.restaurantorsay.com/

(Celebrating at Orsay and getting photobombed by our friend Patrick Wells!)

Why we like it: Without a doubt Orsay is one of our top favorites to go for brunch, lunch, dinner, happy hour, late night menu, or dessert. This is an incredible restaurant with a great bar, lounge dining rooms, and outdoor seating. It's an eclectic crowd of all walks of life, which makes it feel even more city. This is a place to take someone special or to make any day feel like a holiday. I love that I can go wearing yoga clothes or dressed up and feel comfortable either way.

(Mom is pictured with legendary chef and restauranteur, Jonathan Insetta in the lounge area of Orsay.)

What we enjoy here: Everything is fantastic. Mom loves the Beef Stroganoff, the quiches, duck confit cassoulet, croque madam, and hamburgers. I love their olives, cheese and charcuterie, lobster omelet, duck breast, steaks, seafood specials, and meatloaf. The desserts are beyond good and we love the small ones especially as a tower!

Mom says: We always enjoy Orsay and the nice people.

(Mom with Brian Loopuit Mastin at Orsay. Brian said, "I need to approve the photo and make sure I like it before it goes in the book." Mom replies, "Don't worry, if I didn't like you, you wouldn't be going in the book."

(Good times at Sunday Brunch with our sweet friend Hila Head at Orsay.)

Pinegrove Market and Deli

1511 Pine Grove Ave, Jacksonville, FL 32205

(904) 389-8655   http://pinegrovemarket.com/

Why we like it: Super comfortable old school butcher shop and deli vibe. Nice people. High quality everything.

What we enjoy here: We love their burgers and the Cuban sandwich. They sell excellent steaks and will give you perfect cooking instructions.

(Incredible Burger topped with a Fried Egg at Pinegrove Deli.)

Mom says: this is a unique deli and store, and I like it.

South Kitchen & Spirits

3638 Park St, Jacksonville, FL 32205

(904) 475-2362   http://south.kitchen/

Why we like it: Excellent contemporary southern fare in an enjoyable environment. Good service.

What we enjoy here: Pimento cheese, deviled eggs, fried chicken and cobbler. It's consistent and good.

Mom says: I like their fried chicken!

(Incredible Salmon at South Kitchen & Spirits)

The Brick

3585 St Johns Ave, Jacksonville, FL 32205

(904) 387-0606   http://www.brickofavondale.com/

Why we like it: Nice relaxing place in historic Avondale that serves good American cuisine.

What we enjoy here: I love the Salmon and the scallops and the lamb and the steaks. Mom enjoys the chicken cordon blue.

(Mom was thrilled with this meal at The Brick. Who can blame her?)

Mom says: I enjoy coming here and like the bustling environment.

The Fox Restaurant

3580 St Johns Ave, Jacksonville, FL 32205

(904) 387-2669

Why we like it: This amazing old school Avondale institution was revamped by my good friends Ian and Mary Chase in the early 2000s, and it is definitely a worthy destination.

What we enjoy here: Their fried green tomatoes are outstanding, as are their sandwiches, burgers, breakfasts—basically everything you can imagine for a classic good diner. This is updated, classic food.

Mom says: The best! Love the people and good food here.

(What a burger!! You can't beat the Fox!)

(Ian Chase and The Fox: Local Legends)

The Goal Post

3984 Herschel St, Jacksonville, FL 32205

(904) 384-9262

Why we like it: Old School and Amazing sandwich shop. A neighborhood favorite for decades. Vintage Vibes.

What we enjoy here: I love the veggie rider, mom loves the chicken salad. The cream cheese brownie and baklava are radical.

Mom says: Always good. Can't beat a sandwich from here!

Sivada's Cupcakery

3645 St Johns Ave, Jacksonville, FL 32205

(904) 647-7586   https://www.sivadascupcakery.com/

Why we like it: Outstanding gourmet cupcakes. They are so supportive of Orange Park Rotary Club's charity event, *Gourmet Night*.

What we enjoy here: Everything. Especially the almond wedding cake and red Velvet.

Mom says: These cupcakes make any time feel more like a special occasion.

Southern Desert Plate

4205 St Johns Ave, Jacksonville, FL 32210

(904) 388-6400   https://www.southerndessertplate.com/

Why we like it: This wonderful sweet shop with indoor seating is truly outstanding with a wide array of fresh gourmet desserts. It is also located next to what was once Kaldi's—a legendary gourmet market and eatery. It's nice being in this building again having such decadent treats.

What we enjoy here: Mom loves the vanilla cupcake with buttercream icing. I'm a huge fan of the pavlova. I hope to eat my way through their entire menu—and fast!

Mom says: It is a nice environment with friendly people and delicious sweets.

Weise Prescription Shop and Natural Food Shoppe

4343 Colonial Ave Jacksonville, FL 32210

(904) 388-1564   https://www.weiserx.com/the-natural-food-shoppe

Why we like it: I grew up coming here a lot during my childhood with my grandparents or parents and sometimes walking or riding my bike by to get some candied pineapple or yogurt covered almonds. Things that seemed unique and exotic on my way home from Woolworth or playing video games at Aladdin's Castle at the old Roosevelt Mall.

What we enjoy here: Everything they carry is high quality and carefully selected. We recently got some honeycomb to use on a cheese board, chocolate covered almonds, and their famous sesame stick candies. They also make fresh carrot juice and smoothies.

Mom says: I remember coming over here with my mother to get things you couldn't find anywhere else. A very nice store.

Murray Hill

Murry hill is a fantastic old Jacksonville neighborhood that has undergone a resurgence lately. We've always known this is a place to be, and we're so happy about all the new places that have helped to revitalize this wonderful area.

Community Loaves

1120 Edgewood Ave S, Jacksonville, FL 32205

(904) 381-0097   http://communityloavesjax.com/

Why we like it: Homemade independent authentic feel in a comfortable old-fashioned environment. Enjoyable bakery and café.

What we enjoy here: The bread is fresh and delicious. Mom likes to get a grilled cheese here. I like the smoked Salmon sandwich, their salads, and Lemon Lavender Cake with Vanilla Buttercream Icing.

Mom says: This is quality homemade food here.

Edgewood Diner

954 Edgewood Ave S, Jacksonville, FL 32205

(904) 524-8711

Why we like it: Old fashioned diner serving comfort food for breakfast and lunch.

What we enjoy here: Mom likes the waffles and I like the eggs and breakfast offerings

Mom says: A hot waffle and butter is just right.

El Jefe

947 Edgewood Ave S, Jacksonville, FL 32205

(904) 619-0938   https://www.eljefejax.com/

Why we like it: Fun and vibrant Tex Mex spot.

What we enjoy here: Chips and salsas and the combination fajitas are our favorites. Good steak and pork chops too.

Mom says: It is an upbeat place with excellent food and nice people.

(Mom loves the cool vibe and bold colors at El Jefe.)

Grater Goods

1080 Edgewood Ave S #9, Jacksonville, FL 32205

(904) 203-8533   https://gratergoods.com/

Why we like it: This impressive locally-owned, cut and wrap cheese shop is a treasure. They have an impressive array of American and Imported cheeses and charcuterie, jams, pickled vegetables, pecans. The owner, Jennifer, was friendly, knowledgeable, and offered me samples and answered my many questions. This place is our new destination—instead of depending on rides to Gainesville for this level of cheese.

What we enjoy here: I got a wonderful assortment of cheeses and made a board for dinner. The tomato chutney was phenomenal, the wafer crackers area new favorite.

Mom says: So good! Let's pick up some things from here again soon and have another snack dinner.

Maple Street Biscuit Co.

1171 Edgewood Ave S, Jacksonville, FL 32205

(904) 518-4907   https://maplestreetbiscuits.com/

Why we like it: Great local biscuit chain.

What we enjoy here: Mom loves the fried chicken biscuit and I love the barbeque one. Delicious cinnamon raisin for dessert.

Mom says: mmm hmm. Love a good biscuit. Reminds me of Grandma Omie!

(Barbeque biscuit with coleslaw at Maple Street)

Moon River Pizza

1176 Edgewood Ave S, Jacksonville, FL 32205

(904) 389-4442 http://www.moonriverpizza.net/

Why we like it: Casual cool pizza parlor. Major indie with good music playing. Nice people.

What we enjoy here: Pizza! Meat lovers, please.

Mom says: There's nothing better than a good slice when you're hungry, and I'm always hungry.

Dreamette

3646 Post St, Jacksonville, FL 32205

(904) 388-2558

Why we like it: A landmark for all of Florida, especially those of us who grew up in Jacksonville. This cash only soft serve stand is legendary and with good reason.

What we enjoy here: Mom typically likes a chocolate and vanilla twist in a cup but will live it up and have a strawberry dipped in chocolate. I love their vanilla dipped in chocolate but they recently had a sale on double sided cones. The chocolate and vanilla together that way is a real winner. Everything's good here. Great thick shakes too.

Mom says: don't take me here too often I'm eating too much of this delicious ice cream.

Vagabond Coffee

934 Edgewood Ave S, Jacksonville, FL 32205

(904) 402-2373   https://www.vagabondcoffee.com/

Why we like it: So chill and amazing.

What we enjoy here: Everything! Wonderful Ethiopian pour overs. Pop tarts. Quiche and sweet and savory galettes. Fantastic Ginger Molasses cookies.

Mom says: This cookie tastes like an old-fashioned gingerbread man. Yum!

(Delicious homemade sweet and savory baked goods at Vagabond)

Westside

We know it's the Best Side! Just ask us.

Cross Creek Steak House and Ribs

850 Lane Ave S, Jacksonville, FL 32205

(904) 783-9579   http://www.crosscreeksteakhouse.com/

Why we like it: A fun old-fashioned traditional restaurant. Always good.

What we enjoy here: We like the barbeque and all the delicious sides. You can't miss here. Got some nice local honey here too.

Mom says: I love old fashioned good home cooking!

(It's always a good time at Cross Creek!)

Gator's BBQ

8142 West Beaver St, Jacksonville, FL 32220

(904) 683-4941   http://gatorsbbq.net/

Why we like it: One of mom's favorite students from when she taught at W.E. Cherry Elementary in Orange Park, Angela, suggested we try this place, as it's considered by many to have the best barbeque in Jacksonville. It was excellent, the people were friendly, and it's a cute little place with a front porch and has outdoor table where we enjoyed a fine lunch. They moved since we went there, and we look forward to trying the new locations soon.

What we enjoy here: We shared the Fried Squash, which was outstanding, I had great Ribs, Collard Greens, and Macaroni and Cheese, Mom had a Smoked Pork Sandwich, and we both enjoyed the Banana Pudding. Everything was wonderful.

Mom says: This is a good place with nice people. I sure do like their barbeque.

Jacksonville Farmers Market

1810 W Beaver St, Jacksonville, FL 32209

(904) 354-2821   http://jaxfarmersmarket.com/

Why we like it: My mom's father, Henry Strickland "Pappy" came out of retirement twice to help his good friend, Judge Stanley run this market. Some of my earliest memories are of visiting him here and him bringing me watermelons from this incredible place. This is the real deal.

What we enjoy here: There are numerous vendors offering fine fruits, vegetables, honey, syrups, cheeses, breads, muffins, boiled peanuts, coffees, teas, oils, and herbs. We just got some wonderful fresh strawberries here.

Mom says: Now this is truly fresh from the farm. It reminds me of my parents and good times with them.

Lake Shore Produce Market

2326 Blanding Blvd, Jacksonville, FL 32210

(904) 387-1455

Why we like it: This cash-only market has been around for decades and is outstanding. The meats, produce, jarred items, everything is high quality. You can also get Brunswick Stew, Barbeque Chicken, Brisket, Ribs, Macaroni and Cheese, Baked Beans and such for a great meal to go.

What we enjoy here: I have always enjoyed everything I've found at this market—especially the fresh tomatoes, okra, and seasonal fruits and vegetables.

Mom says: This is delicious. I'm okay with picking up from here for lunch in the car or at a nearby park anytime. The picnic table around back is nice too.

Mr. Ed's Heavenly BBQ

5426 Blanding Blvd, Jacksonville, FL 32210

(904) 874-9418   https://mr-eds-heavenly-barbecue.business.site/

Why we like it: A hidden treasure on the Westside. A tiny building with great food.

What we enjoy here: Barbecue and a slice of caramel cake.

Mom says: This cake reminds me of some my aunt used to make in Georgia when I was younger.

Monroe's' Smokehouse Bar-B-Q

Why we like it: It feels like the good old days coming here again, as we used to eat here a lot when it was Pat and Mike's back in the day. The food here is fantastic, it's a nice comfortable place, and the barbeque and side dishes are excellent.

What we enjoy here: We love the ribs and pulled pork. The Macaroni and cheese, collard greens, black eyed peas, sweet Potato casserole, and corn bread are delicious.

Mom says: Wonderful. I want to come back here—soon!

(Mom's pictured with Monroe's owner, Keith Waller, a nice man who's made us feel right at home.)

Soul Food Bistro

5310 Lenox Ave #1, Jacksonville, FL 32205

(904) 394-0860   http://www.thesoulfoodbistro.com/home

Why we like it: Incredible southern soul food cafeteria.

What we enjoy here: I like the fried pork chop, and mom's favorite is the fried chicken. All vegetables, casseroles, and desserts are fresh, generous, and better than usual.

Mom says: This really takes me back to good times.

Ortega

One of our favorite old Jacksonville neighborhoods. Mom's parents used to live near the drawbridge, and we enjoyed a lot of nice times around here with friends and family

The Counter at Carter's Pharmacy

2923 Corinthian Ave, Jacksonville, FL 32210

(904) 389-5558

(The Counter at Carter's: a happy place!)

Why we like it: Total nostalgia and casual fun lunch or treat.

What we enjoy here: We love the chicken salad in a pita. A good mixed cold cut sandwich. There's nothing like a drug store counter. A vanilla or cherry coke is nice too.

Mom says: Sure, I'll have an ice cream cone.

Simply Sara's

2902 Corinthian Ave, Jacksonville, FL 32210

(904) 387-1000   http://simplysaras.net/

(We had the best time closing down Simply Sara's yet again and talking with its owners, and our friends, Sally and James. They're open till 10 on Friday night, which is their Seafood Night, and we often go there for dinner after my Chill-Asana class. It's always incredible!)

Why we like it: Without a doubt Simply Sara's is one of our all-time top favorites. Great food, people, location.

What we enjoy here: Everything. Seafood, crab cakes, fried chicken, grass-fed beef, pork chops, cakes, pies, cobblers, burgers, and pizza. Pimento and cheese and eggplant "fries" are outstanding. (Get a cake or pie for your next holiday, and you'll thank us later!) Brunch, lunch and dinner specials change regularly, and every meal here is a real treat.

(Mom always enjoys Simply Sara's homemade Pimento and Cheese.)

(One of many great dinner's I've enjoyed at this great place)

Mom says: Simply Sara's definitely a favorite! The people are so friendly and down home here. Simply Delicious.

J. L. Trent's Seafood and Grill

4553 120th St, Jacksonville, FL 32244

(904) 908-4202   https://www.jltrents.com/

Why we like it: Casual and consistently good in old Yukon, Florida, near NAS Jax.

What we enjoy here: Fry it up! Seafood spread. Oyster stew. Key lime pie. Oh yeah!

Mom says: MMM. I like this place!

(Happy Birthday lunch for our awesome friend, Laurie Crofton at Trent's Seafood.)

Tumptin Thai Restaurant

5907 Roosevelt Blvd #700, Jacksonville, FL 32244

(904) 619-0406

http://www.tuptimthairestaurantjacksonville.com/

Why we like it: A favorite comfortable and attractive place with nice, professional service.

What we enjoy here: everything is good. Pork, beef, duck, and noodle entrees are traditional and superbly prepared. Chicken Satay, steamed Dumplings and all appetizers are winners too. Their coconut ice cream is the best I've had.

Mom says: I enjoy it here for holidays and a nice dinner.

(My brother took us for an awesome dinner on my birthday last year. Pictured are: Hila Head, Grady H. Williams, Jr. Peggy Allen Williams, Mom, Me, and Joan Tymick-Johnson)

Orange Park

Growing up in this small, charming, and somewhat rural town was wonderful, and I still love it even though it's grown so much. We now have some of the best places around for good food, which is really incredible to me.

Aron's Pizza

650 Park Ave, Orange Park, FL 32073

(904) 269-1007   http://www.aronspizza.com/

Why we like it: Very local feeling and great repurposing of an old Long John Silvers.

What we enjoy here: Excellent pizza. We enjoyed the hamburger style. Good salads and pasta too. The Zepollis with raspberry sauce for dessert are very tempting.

Mom says: Good pizza and close to home. You can't beat it.

(Awesome thin crust BLT pizza at Aron's in Orange Park.)

CamiCakes Cupcakes

1910 Wells Rd, Orange Park, FL 32073

(904) 541-1095   https://www.camicakes.com/

Why we like it: Unexpected over the top cupcakes at the mall. They also have a place in Jacksonville and in the Vinings and Buckhead areas of Atlanta

What we enjoy here: Everything. There is no wrong choice here. Chocolate on yellow is good. Buttercream on yellow is perfect. Chocolate and red Velvet. Get an assortment and try something new. You'll thank us later.

Mom says: Wow! These have a lot of icing, and very rich. Delicious.

The Club Continental

2143 Astor St, Orange Park, FL 32073

(904) 264-6070   https://clubcontinental.com/

Why we like it: This is a historic private dining club and bed and breakfast that plays an important role in the Orange Park community. Guests of the hotel are welcome to dine here, and prospective members can pay using a credit card. There is nowhere more beautiful anywhere; co-owner Karrie Massie has done a stellar job with the grounds. Chef and co-owner Sheldon Harris is a culinary genius, and the brunches, lunches, and dinners we've enjoyed here rival those in any fine restaurant, hotel, or club. There is a beautiful dining room overlooking the St. Johns River, outdoor dining, and a seasonal Cabana by the pools. We don't just like this place: we love it—and the people. This is real Old Florida. Southern and gracious hospitality are hallmarks of this fine establishment. I have served on their board, am a proud member, and hope you'll come for a stay or join too.

What we enjoy here: They do an outstanding job with fresh seafood, steaks, pastas, sandwiches, soups, house-cured meats, and they have a wonderful selection of gourmet desserts.

(Enjoying a wonderful holiday brunch at Club Continental with our good friends, Laurie and Author Crofton)

Mom says: This is a truly beautiful place with excellent food, a gorgeous setting, and the nicest people. Great view!

Famous Sandwiches

862 Blanding Blvd, Orange Park, FL 32065

(904) 579-3151

Why we like it: Consistent local chain that's great for a sandwich hamburger and fries on the go.

What we enjoy here: Camel riders, cheese burgers, and a cherry limeade!

Mom says: A cheeseburger in the car is always fine with me.

Grumpy's Restaurant

834 Kingsley Ave, Orange Park, FL 32073

(904) 215-1956   https://www.grumpysrestaurantco.com/

Why we like it: A casual diner for breakfast and lunch where you're sure to see a lot of locals.

What we like here: We like their breakfast foods and sandwiches the most here.

Mom says: I love their BLT!

G's Slow Smoked BBQ

1282 Blanding Blvd, Orange Park, FL 32065

(904) 406-0524

Why we like it: Excellent barbeque and side dishes. It's top level good stuff.

What we like: We like the feast; and everything here is good. It's a huge selection of great meats and traditional sides.

Mom says: This good food reminds me of the good old days.

The Juicy Crab

8106 Blanding Blvd, Jacksonville, FL 32244

(904) 379-5517   http://www.thejuicycrabjax.com/

Why we like it: An unexpected fun seafood place.

What we enjoy here: The daily special with crab, shrimp, corn, and potatoes is outstanding.

(Having a blast at The Juicy Crab.)

Mom says: It's a little messy eating out of this pot this way, but it sure is good!

The Hilltop Restaurant

2030 Wells Rd, Orange Park, FL 32073

(904) 272-5959   https://the-hilltop-restaurant.business.site/

Why we like it: A somewhat hidden treasure in Orange Park, this is a beautiful restaurant and popular event venue.

What we enjoy here: Wonderful She Crab Soup. Mom likes the pasta, I like the steak or seafood. They do a great job on everything here. Classic desserts such as Red Velvet Cake and Pecan Pie are excellent. Great place for holidays too.

Mom says: This is so nice for a treat or special occasion.

Irie Diner

1177 Park Ave Ste 9, Orange Park, FL 32073

(904) 375-9467   https://www.iriediner.com/

Why we like it: This cheerful place is a welcome addition to Orange Park and is the largest authentic, full-service Caribbean Restaurant in the Jacksonville area. Friendly people and excellent, flavorful food make it a worth destination.

What we enjoy here: We shared the Coconut Shrimp and Sweet Potato Fries as an appetizer, mom had the Curry Chicken, I had the Jamaican Oxtail Stew, and we had the Banana Bread Pudding for dessert. Everything was phenomenal.

Mom says: MMM HMM! This is good!

(Mom is pictured with Irie Diner Owner, Peter Jackson and Chef, Marko Ball who helped us have a great experience.)

The Loop

550 Wells Rd # 1, Orange Park, FL 32073

(904) 269-0756   http://www.looppizzagrill.com/

Why we like it: A favorite local chain, it's always good for a casual bite.

What we enjoy here: Mom loves the tomato bisque, chicken sandwich, and burgers. I am hooked on their kale salad with grilled salmon.

Mom says: You can never go wrong with the Loop!

(Loving it at The Loop!)

Metro Diner

2034 Kingsley Ave, Orange Park, FL 32073

(904) 375-8548

Why we like it: Local chain of diners that is a fan favorite in our area. We love having one in Orange Park but go do different locations too, like San Marco and Roosevelt Mall. They are all good and you can count on a lot of good food and service.

What we enjoy here: Mom loves the Chicken and Waffles and the Chicken Pot Pie. I like the crab cakes and eggs benedict.

(The famous Chicken and Waffles at Metro Diner)

Mom says: I always order too much here, but it is really good fried chicken. The waffle is nice too, especially with this strawberry butter.

Nicole's On The River

1101 Blanding Blvd #117, Orange Park, FL 32065

(904) 251-9977

Why we like it: Casual country cooking cafe that we found because of our friend John Keene at Lucas Honda. This is a true hidden local gem that's worth the drive if you love good old-fashioned Southern style food.

What we enjoy here: Mom had the fried chicken, I had the fried Mayport shrimp. We were both winners. The dessert was a home run too.

(A home run lunch at Nicole's with a happy mom.)

Mom says: It's so nice having a place this good so close by!

OP Fish House & Oyster Bar

636 Kingsley Ave, Orange Park, FL 32073

(904) 579-3931   https://www.opfishhouse.com/

Why we like it: This new addition to the local food scene in Orange Park is most welcome. It's a nice spot for a casual meal of fresh seafood in a historic home that has indoor and outdoor dining.

What we enjoy here: The fish dip is excellent, and we like the fried shrimp and grilled swordfish. We've been pleased with everything we've tried here.

Mom says: It's very nice having another place this good in the actual Town of Orange Park.

Over the Second Cup Tea Room

727 Kingsley Ave., Orange Park, FL 32073

(904) 264-8844   https://www.basketique-gifts.com/

Why we like it: This is a quaint Southern tea room and gift shop that is like taking a step back in time. It is a unique experience and perfect for a ladies luncheon, girl's birthday party, or other special occasion to slow down and enjoy.

What we enjoy here: This six-course tea is a decadent meal that will satisfy hearty appetites. We loved the chilled strawberry soup, fish and chips, sandwiches, scones, and deserts. Everything was fresh and delicious.

Mom (pictured with owner Pat Sessions) says: This is a very special experience and a nice place for my 91st birthday.

The Sheik

1994 Kingsley Ave, Orange Park, FL 32073

(904) 276-2677

Why we like it: Classic and good.

What we enjoy here: Mom loves the chicken salad and the Cheeseburger. I'm a fan of their camel rider or steak in a sack. Cherry Limeade, please!

(I love a good to-go lunch from the Sheik. Camel Rider is my favorite from them always.)

Mom says: umm hmm! Don't forget to get some fries too.

Sorbello's

195 Blanding Blvd, Orange Park, FL 32073

(904) 269-3000   http://www.sorbellosrestaurant.com/

Why we like it: outstanding Sicilian food with very nice people. An Orange Park favorite for about 20 years.

What we enjoy here: outstanding pasta, rolls, and nice low carb options. Everything is fantastic.

Mom says: I enjoy these nice people as much as the great meals.

(Our family loves celebrating at Sorbello's! Me, Peggy Williams, Allen Strickland Williams, Mom, Aziz and Allison Coleman, and Grady H. Williams, Jr.)

Sam's St Johns Seaford

4908, 1464 Park Ave, Orange Park, FL 32073

(904) 269-1460   https://www.lovethatseafood.com/Home

Why we like it: One of our favorite local spots since the mid-80s. Love the food and the people!

What we enjoy here: Crab legs, fried seafood, pasta, grilled Mahi, Okra and Tomatoes, steak, and homemade key lime and peanut butter pies.

Mom says: I always enjoy it here and it just feels homey.

The Granary

1738 Kingsley Ave, Orange Park, FL 32073

(904) 269-7222   http://www.thegranarywholefoods.com/

Why we like it: A natural foods market forerunner.

What we enjoy here: Excellent organic produce, eggs, honey, bread, packaged foods and soups.

Mom says: Such a nice local shop we've enjoyed for many years.

Tom and Betty's

2134 Park Ave, Orange Park, FL 32073

(904) 375-1965   https://www.tomandbettys.net/

Why we like it: This almost 50-year-old Jacksonville landmark relocated to Orange Park recently, and we are so glad it did.

What we enjoy here: Insane sandwiches and homemade pie. Mom had a huge club style and I did the Shaved Ribeye Steak sandwich. We shared pecan pie. We both had to go boxes and another meal (or two).

Mom says: This is just one sandwich?! Delicious!

Urban Bean Coffeehouse Cafe

2023 Park Ave, Orange Park, FL 32073

(904) 541-4938   http://www.theurbanbeancoffeehouse.com/

Why we like it: A favorite coffee shop café that we can't believe is in Orange Park. We'd drive across the universe for this place. It reminds us of our good friends Josh Dupree who loved it too and Melissa who we had fun here with. This is a place to really enjoy with friends and family. A charming environment owned and operated by the nicest family and wonderful staff. Feels like home away from home.

What we enjoy here: Pour over coffees. Incredible donuts, grass-fed burgers, cheese and charcuterie, brie and apple sandwich. Great cookies! Mom loves the red velvet with white chocolate chips.

Mom says: Are we really in Orange Park?

(Loving a late lunch on the patio with Mom at Urban Bean)

(A happy time with our friends Russell Moore and Melissa Ball. We miss Melissa but cherish these memories.)

(Enjoying a volunteer meeting for Grace Episcopal Church with my friends Linda and Bill Spencer. The Urban Bean is a meeting place for many of people to enjoy and be productive).

Vito's Pizzeria

1101 Blanding Blvd # 112, Orange Park, FL 32065

(904) 272-9119   http://www.vitosorangepark.com/

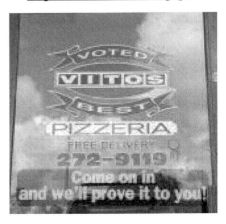

Why we like it: Outstanding pizza. Some of the best around.

What we enjoy here: We love the White and Meat Lover's Pizzas.

(Great meat lovers and white pizzas from Vitos Pizzeria!)

Mom says: This here is some really good pizza.

Fleming Island

Once like a wilderness, this beautiful area of Clay County is now booming.

Brick Oven Pizza and Gastropub

1811 Town Center Blvd, Fleming Island, FL 32003

(904) 278-1770   http://www.brickovengastropub.com/

Why we like it: Excellent local spot with top notch pizzas.

What we enjoy here: We love the White Pizza, the Vegan, and the Pepperoni.

Mom says: I want some more pizza from this place soon!

(White Pizza from Brick Oven and a salad by Andrea Hernandez at our Yoga Den Fleming Island family dinner.)

Margaritas

3535 US-17 #8, Fleming Island, FL 32003

(904) 375-9395   http://margaritasflemingisland.com/

Why we like it: Great casual Mexican restaurant with outstanding food and service. Plus, it's in the same shopping center as Yoga Den Fleming Island!

What we enjoy here: Excellent guacamole, chips, salsa, fajitas, burritos, salads, quesadillas, carnitas, chicken, beef, and churros.

(Our friendly server, Lina making a gray day a lot nicer as she prepares fresh Guacamole tableside for us!)

Mom says: Having somewhere this good this close is really nice, but I have to be careful here. It's all too good.

Santioni's Italian Restaurant

3535 US-17, Fleming Island, FL 32003

(904) 264-1331   https://santionis.com/

Why we like it: Outstanding Italian cuisine in a nice upscale environment.

What we enjoy here: Mom loves the Tortellini Ala Pana, and I love the steak, lamb, Chicken Cacciatore. Everything is stellar.

Mom says: I was proud to have my 90th birthday party here last year.

(Mom with her favorite pasta dinner at Santioni's)

Time Out Deli & Grill

4311 US-17, Orange Park, FL 32003

(904) 637-0012

Why we like it: This place is the epitome of a hole-in-the-wall local treasure. It's right next to a gas station and convenience shop on 17, near where I teach at Fleming Island, and I've driven by it many times. Friends recommended it recently, and it is a real find. Great casual, classic breakfast and lunch sandwich shop type of place that specializes in Middle Eastern Cuisine. Great for dine in or take out. Very local feel.

What we enjoy here: Mom loves their Chicken Salad in a Pita, I love the Camel Rider and Cherry Limeade, we both love the fries and Baklava

Mom says: I like getting a sandwich here and eating it in the park.

Whitey's Fish Camp

2032 County Rd 220, Fleming Island, FL 32003

(904) 269-4198   http://www.whiteysfishcamp.com/

Why we like it: Down home authentic southern fish camp. Real Florida setting with great food, beautiful view, and local crowd.

What we enjoy here: Fried fare is good here, and they have great oysters and bar. Their smoked fish spread is truly incredible. Excellent fried shrimp, catfish, soft-shell crab. Nice indoor and outdoor seating areas for dining and bar patrons.

Mom says: It's so country feeling here, and good eats. I like it a lot!

Green Cove Springs

A charming little town in Clay County that we love.

D'Fontana

324 Ferris St, Green Cove Springs, FL 32043

(904) 529-5515

Why we like it: Small unpretentious with excellent Italian fare.

What we enjoy here: Mom loves the pasta and pizza, and my favorite is the Chicken Francaise.

(D'Fontana's Chicken Francaise is some of the best I've had.)

Mom says: Such a charming little place with the best food.

Farmers in the Deli

810 N Orange Ave, Green Cove Springs, FL 32043

(904) 671-3325

Why we like it: Cute small sandwich shop café with nice people. Located right across the street from the beautiful Clay County Courthouse, this is a favorite spot to see a lot of locals and enjoy a scenic view too.

What we enjoy here: We love the sandwiches and the meatloaf. Excellent homemade desserts.

Mom says: This is my kind of casual place.

Spring Park Coffee

328 Ferris St, Green Cove Springs, FL 32043

(904) 531-9391   http://www.springparkcoffee.com/

Why we like it: A favorite place to relax in the comfortable setting filled with antique furniture. Friendly people.

What we enjoy here: Brass Tacks coffee, mom loves the cane colas, breakfast sandwiches, cakes, and cookies.

Mom says: I've never had Funfetti cake before, but I like it!

Sweet Sensations

25 N Orange Ave, Green Cove Springs, FL 32043

(904) 529-8554

Why we like it: Outstanding and consistent casual sandwich shop/bakery/café.

What we enjoy here: Shepperd's Pie, Cuban Sandwich, soups, cakes, pies, and cookies. All fantastic here.

Mom says: What a comfortable old-fashioned place!

(Excellent Pies, Sandwiches, Soups at Sweet Sensations make this a great place to visit in Green Cove Springs.)

Middleburg

The fact that Middleburg has a few of the best places we've visited during the work on Good Eats Jax is something I'm happy to report. We love this little country town and enjoy these great restaurants.

Nicole's in the Country

2216 S Mimosa Ave, Middleburg, FL 32068

(904) 406-9491

(Mom absolutely loved the ride out here to Nicole's in the Country and had a great time at this excellent little café.)

Why we like it: This place is comfortable, literally in the country, very nice people, and outstanding food. It doesn't get any better than this.

What we enjoy here: These are some of the best fried Mayport shrimp I've ever had, and they really take me back to my childhood. Mom loves the fried chicken.

(One of the nicest things that's happened on our work on Good Eats Jax was meeting Gerald Beasley and talking with him about how we used to have dinner at his old restaurant, The Rite Spot almost every Saturday night for years in Mayport with our family when I was little. He showed us the old sign and treated me and mom like family and suggested we revive our weekly dinner tradition here. I hope we will.)

Mom says: It's like the Rite Spot moved out to the country. These are nice people serving really good food. I hope we come back here soon.

(The old Rite Spot sign at Nicole's in the Country)

Royal Moose Coffee Co.

2441 Blanding Blvd, Middleburg, FL 32068

(904) 406-0661

Why we like it: This is an unexpected locally-owned free-standing newer coffee shop with a drive through window and tables outside. It's absolutely incredible with friendly service. We enjoyed talking with the owner and our server. Hope to visit here often.

What we like: Mom had a cheeseburger on a croissant, and I had an outstanding hot Chicken Croissant with Ham and Bacon and a fine cup of black coffee.

Mom says: This is a great cheeseburger!

Spice

2475 Blanding Blvd #7, Middleburg, FL 32068

(904) 290-2660   https://spice-club.co/

Why we like it: One of the best surprises of our culinary expedition through North Florida was finding this dramatic international eatery in a strip mall on Blanding Blvd. in Middleburg. They offer an eclectic mix of world cuisine, and it is very good, cooked-to order. You can also call ahead to order an excellent to-go meal.

What we enjoy here: Mom loves the Chicken Snitzel and German Potato Salad. I think their Ribeye is one of the finest I've had anywhere. We both enjoy the Vanilla Pot du Crème.

Mom says: It takes some time to have them cook your meal fresh for you, and it's worth the wait.

Mandarin

Now a super busy part of town, Mandarin still has an old Florida charm we love.

Berndt Ends BBQ

10131 San Jose Blvd, Jacksonville, FL 32257

(904) 379-0222

Why we like it: This place is a real winner. Literally, Shane Berndt has won numerous BBQ contests and is know for his innovate use of Datil Peppers. Nice people, super fresh food, and a casual environment with picnic tables make it an easy-going place for lunch or dinner. They cook a limited amount each day, and when they sell out, that's that until the next day.

What we enjoy here: Ribs, Sausage, Turkey, Pork, Beef, Greens, Beans, Macaroni, and Banana Pudding and Blueberry Cobbler Ice Creams. Everything is excellent.

Mom says: Great BBQ and people. I like coming here.

Clarks Fish Camp Seafood Restaurant

12903 Hood Landing Rd, Jacksonville, FL 32258

(904) 268-3474   http://www.clarksfishcamp.net/

Why we like it: You don't get any more real old Florida than this place. Rustic and awesome on many levels.

What we enjoy here: We love their fish spread as an appetizer, Mom loved the shrimp and grit cakes, and I am crazy over their low country boil. The key lime pie was perfect.

Mom says: Someone put a lot of thought into displaying all these animals and things. So neat!

Don Juan's Restaurant

12373 San Jose Blvd, Jacksonville, FL 32223

(904) 268-8722   http://www.donjuansjax.com/

Why we like it: A reliable and popular Mandarin favorite for Mexican food.

What we enjoy here: We loved the fajitas and will be back for more soon.

Mom says: A really busy place with lots of nice people all around.

(Very generous serving of Fajita's at Don Juan's)

Enza's

10601 San Jose Blvd #109, Jacksonville, FL 32257

(904) 268-4458   https://www.enzas.net/

Why we like it: It's a comfortable place in a strip mall setting that offers some outstanding Italian cuisine.

What we enjoy here: Mom loves their fettuccini, and I love their fresh seafood specials.

Mom says: Now this is some good pasta!

(Incredible Scallops at Enza's!)

Good Chi Coffee

8789 San Jose Blvd., Jacksonville, FL 32217

https://www.facebook.com/goodchicoffee/

(Mom's pictured with owner, Chip Foreacre who, with his wife, Alyson Foreacre, also own Yoga Den, where I teach.)

Why we like it: This new addition to the local coffee shop scene offers Brass Tacks Coffee, wraps and salads from Native Sun and desserts from Amaretti Bakery. Conveniently located in San Jose Park, and adjacent to the Yoga Den Studio, there's a lot of seating and an awesome community vibe.

What we enjoy here: Everything. Mom likes the hot chocolate, and I like a nice pour over coffee.

Mom says: This is a nice place to enjoy time with friends.

Hoby's Honey & General Store

11362 San Jose Blvd unit 13, Jacksonville, FL 32223

(904) 701-4769

Why we like it: The people were so welcoming and nice to us that it set an immediate positive vibe. This locally-sourced *old fashioned store has lot of good honeys, preserves, pickled* vegetables, olives, and assorted goods and gift items from Jacksonville-area vendors such as Topsy Toffee, Chef Phil's BBQ Sauce, FreshJax Spices & Salts, and Hyppo Pops.

What we enjoy here: We got some great spicy peach jam that we put on brie and blue cheese stuffed olives we used on a cheese board. Everything is excellent.

Mom (pictured with owner Ryan Hoback) says: They make you feel like you're a friend visiting. These are nice people you want to get to know with a lovely store.

Julington Creek Fish Camp

12760 San Jose Blvd, Jacksonville, FL 32223

(904) 886-2267   https://julingtoncreekfishcamp.com/

Why we like it: An upscale fish camp that always exceeds our expectations. We love the food, view, and service here. They also have two other great locations: Atlantic Beach and Palm Valley.

(Mom branching out and having the fried chicken here and loving it!)

What we enjoy here: The steamed shrimp and crab cakes are excellent. I love their fresh catch specials and mom loves the shrimp salad sandwich and the fried chicken. Decadent desserts are worth a try here too. We especially love the key lime pie.

Mom says: It's so cheerful and beautiful here.

Kazu Japanese Restaurant

9965 San Jose Blvd #35, Jacksonville, FL 32257

(904) 683-9903   http://www.kazujapaneserestaurant.com/

Why we like it: Excellent Japanese fare.

What we enjoy here: Mom likes the tempura and I love the sushi.

Mom says: The food is so light and flavorful here.

(Delicious salad. Everything is done well at Kazu.)

Kim's Korean BBQ Restaurant

9825 San Jose Blvd #1, Jacksonville, FL 32257

(904) 619-5832

Why we like it: An exotic experience and a delicious one too.

What we enjoy here: Everything was good, but we aren't totally clear on what it all was. The beef dishes were great.

(An assortment of little delicacies at Kim's)

Mom says: This is very different for me, but it's also very good. You can learn a lot of new things going to different places like this.

Mama Q's

10550 Old St Augustine Rd #6, Jacksonville, FL 32257

(904) 260-6262   http://mamaqspizza.com/

Why we like it: One of the nicest surprises in this culinary adventure was finding this quaint pizzeria in a strip mall in Mandarin.

What we enjoy here: The Loaded Mashed Potato Pizza was phenomenal.

Mom says: Such a cute little place with great pizza!

Native Sun Natural Foods Market

10000 San Jose Blvd, Jacksonville, FL 32257

(904) 260-6950   https://www.nativesunjax.com/

Why we like it: Lunch here is one of our favorite things. They also have great locations at Baymeadows and Jax Beach.

What we enjoy here: The wraps, salads, sandwiches, juices, smoothies, shrimp salad, deli items, and soups are so good.

Mom says: It's nice eating in a store like this where everything is such high quality. Very nice.

(Mom's enjoying one of her favorite lunches at Native Sun: a wrap, soup, and Taro chips!)

Le Petit Paris French Café

9965 San Jose Blvd., Jacksonville FL 32257

(904) 512-7777 www.leptitparisjax.com

Why we like it: An authentic French café in Mandarin with a nice relaxed feel, this place delicious classic fare.

What we enjoy here: Mom enjoys the quiche, and I love the smoked salmon and prosciutto and goat cheese salads. The macarons, Nutella croissant donut, Pain au Chocolat, and Triple Berry Tart are all fresh and fantastic.

Mom says: This is an easy going, everyday kind of place where they make you feel special.

(Mom is pictured with owner, Alex Chezaud who has made us feel very welcome on this charming café.)

Picasso's

10503 San Jose Blvd, Jacksonville, FL 32257

(904) 880-0811

https://jaxpicassos.wixsite.com/jaxpicassos

Why we like it: This is one of our absolute, all-time favorite restaurants. It is casual, packed, fresh, delicious, and consistent with nice people. Chef Chris Evan's food is truly incredible. It's a real treat to eat here.

What we enjoy here: Great pizza, Fettucine with grilled chicken, sandwiches, salads, steak specials, fresh catch, barbeque shrimp, and homemade desserts. Orange Crunch Cake!

Mom (enjoying her first Kentucky Hot Brown Sandwich) says: You have to be patient while they cook your dinner and it's worth the wait.

(One of many large and incredible steaks I've had at Picassos and their Spicy Pasta Arrabiata. Just incredible.)

(Incredible fresh catch at Picasso's: Golden Tile with Braised Kale and Sweet Potato Hash. The always have an excellent fresh catch special.)

Season's Bakery and Dumplings

10584-10 Old St Augustine Rd, Jacksonville, FL 32257

(904) 465-5155   http://seasonsdumpling.com/

Why we like it: A fun new addition to the Mandarin area, this Taiwanese eatery is casual, reasonably priced, and delicious.

(Mom trying new things at Season's)

What we enjoy here: We love the noodle dishes, dumplings, and the Matca Cheesecake.

Mom says: Very flavorful and the people are lovely here.

Tillman's Meats & Country Store

10177 Old St Augustine Rd, Jacksonville, FL 32257

(904) 268-1535   https://www.tillmanscountrystore.com/

Why we like it: Old fashioned meat shop with lots of bottled sodas, jams, fresh-picked vegetables, candies, and they do barbeque on the weekend.

What we enjoy here: It's a fun experience. Everything we've purchased here has been great, and we're going for the cookout soon.

Mom says: I love this country place!

V Pizza

12601 San Jose Blvd, Jacksonville, FL 32223

(904) 647-9424   https://www.vpizza.com/

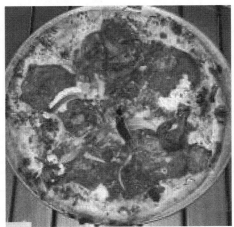

Why we like it: A fun environment, great pizza, and gelato.

What we enjoy here: The chicken wing pizza is amazing.

Mom says: Get a box. We're not wasting any of this!

Fruit Cove

This growing area south of Julington Creek and north of St. Augustine has become a favorite destination as well as drive to and from other parts of town.

Belgium Sweet House

445 State Rd 13 #5, Fruit Cove, FL 32259

(904) 703-4021   https://belgian-sweet-house.business.site/

Why we like it: This remarkable place serves sweet and savory crepes, European sandwiches, and Belgian waffles and has an incredible assortment of confections.

What we enjoy here: We loved the fresh fruit crepe and Belgian waffle with chocolate, whipped cream, and fresh strawberries. Their chocolates are handmade and are some of the best I've had anywhere in the U.S. or Europe.

Mom (pictured with owner, Chantal) says: I can't believe how good everything is and how generous the servings are.

Blackstone Grill

112 Bartram Oaks Walk #102, Fruit Cove, FL 32259

(904) 287-0766

Why we like it: Elegant white-linen restaurant that serves delicious lunch and dinner. A respite from hectic life, traffic, and makes any day a good one. Asian American. Wonderful. Helen and hèr staff make you feel valued and welcome.

What we like here: Everything is good. Lamb, Steak, Chicken, Salads, Barbeque Bacon Wrapped Shrimp, Sushi, Decadent Desserts, like the White Chocolate Mousse below.

Mom says: This place is really very nice and relaxing.

Iggy's

104 Bartram Oaks Walk #101, Fruit Cove, FL 32259

(904) 209-5209 http://iggysgrill.com/

Why we like it: A good casual spot in the Bartram Walk Shopping center on the corner of 13 and Racetrack Road.

What we enjoy here: Mom loves the hamburger, the Grilled Brie and Lobster is insanely good, and we enjoyed the seafood nachos.

Mom says: Iggy? I have never seen so much delicious food.

The Poppin Box

116 Bartram Oaks Walk #102, St Johns, FL 32259

(904) 484-7030   http://www.thepoppinbox.com/

Why we like it: Fun old-fashioned candy and popcorn store with fudge, vintage sodas and other novelties.

What we enjoy here: the beer cheese, the zebra, and the salted caramel popcorn are delicious. They have a lot of flavors available in a variety of sizes.

Mom says: This Poppin Box is so cute with nice people.

Twisted Compass

585 SR 13 - 101, St Johns, FL 32259

(904) 217-0916   https://twistedcompassbrewing.com/

Why we like it: A cool place to hang out, have a treat, relax, or get some work done.

What we enjoy here: The Knead baked goods and Bold Bean coffee are always a treat.

Mom says: So glad we found this place!

(Mom matching the interior Twisted Compass Brewing Co.)

Vito's Italian Restaurant

116 Bartram Oaks Walk #101, Jacksonville, FL 32259

(904) 429-3868   http://www.vitosoriginalitalian.com/

Why we like it: Excellent classic Italian with professional service.

What we enjoy here: The bread and salads are fresh and tasty, and mom loves their tortellini. I enjoyed the chicken Francaise. The bread and salads were superb too.

Mom says: Wonderful!

St. Johns / Switzerland

If you head down south past Julington Creek and Fruit Cove on State Road 13, you'll enjoy one of the most beautiful drives in our area. This area is scenic and also developing.

Adam's Heritage Market

2040 SR 13, Switzerland, Florida 32259

Why we like it: This small old grocery store and with a front porch reminds me of my Dad's Aunt Rebe's Williams Grocery in Athens, Georgia. This is like being on the TV Show the Walton's. It's a quaint place with nice people, fresh produce, breads, baked goods, jams, honey, rice, teas and coffees.

What we enjoy here: We always find great unique things here and recently got some delicious Peach Butter here and Chocolate Covered Peanuts.

Mom says: I like riding through the country to come to this nice store.

Arlington / Southside / Town Center / Baymeadows

There's a lot going on in these spread out parts of town and fortunately great local spots all over.

Bambino Scoops – Gelato

2771 Monument Rd #36, Jacksonville, FL 32225

(904) 566-7149   https://www.bambinoscoops.com/

Why we like it: Charming gelato and dessert shop.

What we enjoy here: Strawberry for mom and cookies and cream for me.

Mom says: I'm glad this place is way across town or I'd want to come here too much!

Beach Road Chicken Dinners

4132 Atlantic Blvd, Jacksonville, FL 32207

(904) 398-7980

Why we like it: A Jacksonville Institution

What we enjoy here: Fried chicken, creamed peas, mashed potatoes and gravy, biscuits, and peach cobbler.

Mom says: This is some *really* good fried chicken!

(We're always happy to make it to Beach Road Chicken Dinners—a true Jacksonville institution.)

Blue Bamboo

3820 Southside Blvd, Jacksonville, FL 32216

(904) 646-1478   https://bluebamboojacksonville.com/

Why we like it: One of our very favorite places. We love Blue Bamboo and Chef Dennis. Great people and food here. Always nice seeing Mr. Chan too.

(Wrapping up a spectacular New Year's Eve dinner with homemade Chocolate Lava Cake at Blue Bamboo.)

What we enjoy: Homerun everything. Lives up to the Hip Asian Comfort Food description. Love Dim Sum Brunch, Ramen Night, and lunch or dinner any day. Lobster, Pork Ribeye, Ribs, Noodles, Crispy Sweet and Sour Chicken. It's the best of the best for classic Chinese and updated classics. Get dessert! Green Tea Crème Brule, Mini Donuts. His award-winning Orange Crunch Cake is worth the splurge.

Mom says: Our friends here are the Chef and his father, and we enjoy the nice servers a lot. They make what is already a very nice place even more special. I really like coming here a lot!

(Chef Dennis Chan, Mom, and me planning the Good Eats Jax book launch party at Blue Bamboo. Dennis has become a good friend, and we met him though our wonderful friend, Judy Wells. Both have done much to help us with this project. Thank you!)

Bono's Pit BAR-B-Q

10065 Skinner Lake Dr, Jacksonville, FL 32246

(904) 998-1997   http://www.bonosbarbq.com/

Why we like it: For about 60 years Bono's has been a Jacksonville go-to for good barbeque and it's still that way. We love this one at the Town Center because it's fun to sit outside. They are all over and all good.

Why we like it: I love their turkey and mom loves the pork.

Mom says: It's always so tender, flavorful, and good!

(Picnic dinner at Bono's at the Town Center!)

Bowl of Pho

9902 Old Baymeadows Rd, Jacksonville, FL 32256

(904) 646-4455

Why we like it: Casual, interesting, and good place in Deerwood shopping center for big bowls of Pho and other Vietnamese cuisine.

What we enjoy here: I had the Pho and mom had fried rice. Both were outstanding.

Mom says: I love trying different places like this. So wonderful that we have so many options these days.

5th Element Indian Restaurant

9485 Baymeadows Rd, Jacksonville, FL 32256

(904) 448-8265   http://www.5thelementindian.com/

Why we like it: An authentic Indian buffet with a wide array of classics that is fresh, delicious, and with friendly service.

What we enjoy here: We enjoyed everything we tried. Great Naan, chutneys, curries, potato dishes. Mom loved the mango soft serve ice cream.

Mom says: These dishes are flavorful and very good here.

Full Circle Eatery

8101 Philips Hwy, Jacksonville, FL 32256

(904) 503-3829   http://www.fullcircleeatery.com/

Why we like it: A true hidden gem in the Avonlea Antique Mall on the corner or Phillips and Baymeadows, this café is top notch with excellent service.

What we enjoy here: Everything is outstanding. First rate versions of classic desserts, sandwiches. We love trying whatever is fresh or on special. It's all excellent.

Mom says: "Keep that pie away from me!"

(Incredible desserts at Full Circle Eatery!)

Gilbert's Social

4021 Southside Blvd #200, Jacksonville, FL 32216

(904) 647-7936   http://www.gilbertssocial.co/

Why we like it: Soul food at its best.

What we enjoy here: The barbeque and fried chicken are standouts. Everything is excellent. The southern bowls are wonderful. I enjoyed their beef stroganoff.

Mom says: You get a lot of flavor and a lot of food at Gilbert's!

JJ's Bistro De Paris

7643 Gate Pkwy #105, Jacksonville, FL 32256

(904) 996-7557   https://www.jjbistro.com/

Why we like it: Parisian themed eatery that serves outstanding and authentic classic French Cuisine. Consistent and excellent, friendly service. Our favorite server, Jody, makes us feel like old friends. Wonderful times here.

What we enjoy here: Mom loves the creme Brule here and the beef bourbon. I love the duck confit. Wonderful fresh Fruit tart, macarons. Everything is spot on.

Mom says: I love coming here and the people make you feel good too.

(Enjoying our time at JJ's, as always.)

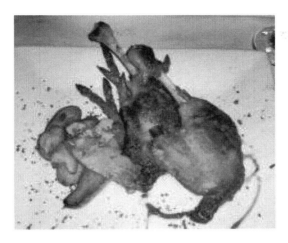

(Perfect Duck Confit at JJ's)

(One of the nicest things about working on the Good Eats Jax and book is meeting so many nice people and making new friends. Mom is pictured with Jodi who's such a great server and fun to talk with. Supporting local, and enjoying delicious food is wonderful, but it's really the people who make this project such a positive experience.)

M Shack

10281 Mid Town Pkwy, Jacksonville, FL 32246

(904) 642-5000   http://www.mshackburgers.com/

Why we like it: One of our favorite spots by far, and we especially like eating outside just hanging out in the parking lot taking it all in. There's a lot to watch and enjoy. You order, and they serve you. Full bar area too.

What we enjoy here: Mom loves the Crab Cake Burger or Chicken Sandwich. I love the CrossFit Burger. We usually share a Kale Salad and order of Sweet Potato Tots. They also have excellent Milk Shakes.

Mom says: I just enjoy relaxing here. It's easy going, and consistently good.

Mambos Cuban Café

13770 Beach Blvd #9, Jacksonville, FL 32224

(904) 374-2046   https://mamboscubancafe.com/

(Enjoying Flan at Mambo's)

Why we like it: Wonderful Cuban food.

What we enjoy here: We shared an outstanding shrimp appetizer. Mom had the chicken and rice and I had the pork. Everything was perfect. Great service. The Flan was memorable.

Mom says: I didn't realize I liked Flan this much!

Medierranea Restaurant

3877 Baymeadows Rd, Jacksonville, FL 32217

(904) 731-2898   http://mediterraniarestaurant.com/

Why we like it: Comfortable Greek standby for decades.

What we enjoy here: We love the humus with pita, the grape leaves, mom loves the pasta alfredo, I love the Lamb.

Mom says: So relaxed and so good!

TimWah Chinese Dim Sum Restaurant

8358 Point Meadows Dr suite 11, Jacksonville, FL 32256

(904) 329-3676   https://www.timwahdimsum.com/

Why we like it: Excellent Dim Sum brought around to you on a cart. Reminds me of China Town in London.

(Wonderful Dim Sum options abound at TimWah.)

What we enjoy here: As much Dim Sum as we can manage to eat!

Mom says: I always love a snack dinner, and these are tasty.

Moxie Kitchen + Cocktails

4972 Big Island Drive, Jacksonville, FL 32246

(904) 998-9744   https://www.moxiefl.com/

(One of the best views in town and caught a candid shot of one of the best (and nicest) chefs anywhere. We love Moxie!)

Why we like it: A definite favorite opened by genius chef Tom Gray, this modern building at the Town Center is a culinary oasis.

What we enjoy here: Deviled Eggs, Smoked Fish Dip with Lavash, Fried Cheese Curds, Brussels Sprouts, Trout Almandine, Fried Chicken and Waffles, Hamburgers, Steak. You can't go wrong for lunch, brunch, dinner, cocktails, or dessert at this incredible restaurant.

(Pimento and Cheese on Toasts and Deviled Eggs at Moxie)

Mom (pictured with Owner and Chef Tom Gray) says, I always enjoy coming to Moxie. Such a treat!

Natural Life

4818 River City Dr, Jacksonville, FL 32246

(904) 997-7772   https://www.naturallife.com/

(Me and good friend and co-god parent to Nathan and Charlotte Reeder, Jane Hughes and checking out the tasty local treats at Natural Life's super cute store at the Town Center--one of only a few locally-owned stores in that area!)

Why we like it: This locally owned shop has and is a wonderful place to visit. They have the Fearless collection to benefit local partner OCD Jacksonville, to connect people who are struggling with obsessive compulsive disorder and anxiety with the best mental health treatment options.

What we enjoy here: Hyppo Pops and other sweet treats.

Mom says: I like coming here to sit, relax, and talk to the nice people.

Pho Dim Sum

9866-8, Baymeadows Rd, Jacksonville, FL 32256

(904) 619-4606

Why we like it: We love Dim Sum, and theirs is great!

What we enjoy here: We tried an assortment and had a bowl of Pho each. Everything was outstanding.

Mom says: We need to come back here for the good food and nice people.

(We enjoyed delicious food and excellent service in this family owned restaurant. Our server, Jasmine made it a great visit, and we will be back soon to enjoy another meal at Pho Dim Sum.)

Atlantic / Neptune / Jacksonville Beaches

These three areas consist of what people typically refer to as the Jacksonville Beaches area. They offer a wide array of casual and fine dinning for locals and tourists alike. You won't be disappointed with any of these new or established eateries and hope you enjoy your time at the beaches as much as we do.

Buddha's Belly

301 10th Ave N, Jacksonville Beach, FL 32250

(904) 372-9149   http://www.buddhathaibistro.com/

Why we like it: Excellent Thai restaurant. Nice environment and good service. Lots of great vegan options here.

What we enjoy here: We tried some appetizers and different curries. Everything was great, as was the chocolate dessert.

Mom says: I'm getting spoiled eating all this good food!

Catullo's Italian

1650-2 San Pablo Rd. S, Jacksonville, Florida 32225

Why we like it: I don't just say this lightly: Our dinner here was one of the best of my life. When I lived in New York my favorite meal was the tortellini with smoked salmon and caviar at Cafe Bianco on the Upper East Side. This Pear Fiocchi reminds me of loving a pasta dinner that much.

What we enjoy here: The crispy risotto balls with goat cheese were a great appetizer with a real kick from the chili. Mom loved here carbonara and I was completely blown away by the Pear Fiocchi. The bread was hot, fresh, delicious. The Lemoncello Mascarpone Cake was superb, and the Chocolate

Bombe was, well, the bomb. This meal was so worth the cheat. Great environment and friendly, professional, and attentive service. This was a home-run experience.

Mom says: I can't keep eating like this. It's so good!

Cinotti's Bakery and Sandwich Shop

1523 Penman Rd, Jacksonville Beach, FL 32250

(904) 246-1728 https://cinottisbakery.com/

Why we like it: Amazing Old School Bakery. A beaches institution.

What we enjoy here: Cookies, cakes, and Pumpkin Donuts.

Mom says: A lot of old-fashioned goodness here!

(Mom felt right at home at Cinotti's)

Dwight's Mediterranean Style Bistro

1527 Penman Rd, Jacksonville Beach, FL 32250

(904) 241-4496   http://www.dwightsbistro.com/

Why we like it: Beyond expectations. Great people, service, food. Cool tile work by Dwight too.

What we enjoy here: Crab Cakes, Pasta, and the mixed grill were all excellent. The Bananas Foster is incredible!

Mom says: Outstanding!

(We had an outstanding dinner at Dwight's. It's a first-class experience on all levels.)

The Fish Company

725-12 Atlantic Blvd, Atlantic Beach, FL 32233

(904) 246-0123   https://thefishcojax.com/

Why we like it: A casual beach place with excellent fresh seafood.

What we enjoy here: We shared a scallop appetizer. Mom had a lightly blackened Mahi, and I had a broth bowl special with fresh fish. It was excellent. The Key Lime Pie was delicious.

Mom says: I don't know how you found this place, but I'm glad you did.

Gilbert's Southern Kitchen + Bar

831 1st St N, Jacksonville Beach, FL 32250

(904) 372-0444   https://www.gilbertssouthern.com/

Why we like it: Beautiful outdoor dining overlooking the ocean with Chef Gilbert's excellent BBQ and southern sides.

What we enjoy here: The Pimento Cheese and Boiled **Peanuts, Mixed Meat BBQ Platter, and Banana Pudding.**

Mom says: I don't know when I've had so much fun or tasted such good food. Our server was extra nice and attentive. I love being out by the beach too.

House of Leaf and Bean

14474 Beach Blvd, Jacksonville, FL 32250

(904) 379-1291   https://www.houseofleafnbean.com/

Why we like it: This is an innovative place serving fresh organic foods, with excellent teas, and a Zen room. It is

What we enjoy here: We loved the Edamame Garbanzo Hummus, Handmade Golden Dumplings, California Salad, and the Chicken Zen Bowl.

Mom (pictured with owner, Wan Raiti) says: Everything is so delicious and what nice people! I want to come back here.

Marker 32

14549 Beach Blvd, Jacksonville, FL 32250

(904) 223-1534   https://marker32.com/

Why we like it: One of my favorites since the 90s and one of the best fine dining places in town. Wonderful view too.

What we enjoy here: Mom had a huge Pork Chop, and I had a major steak. We were very happy and had a big lunch with our leftovers the next day.

Mom says: This is a very special occasion place. I like it.

The Mini Bar

1300 Beach Blvd, Jacksonville Beach, FL 32250

https://minibardonuts.com/

Why we like it: Super cute and trendy donut place at the beach.

What we enjoy here: The small cake donuts are served warm with toppings made to order. We enjoyed the Maple Bacon, Coffee Cake, and Fruity Pebbles.

Mom says: Warm, delicious, and dangerous for your diet.

(Mini Bar is definitely a treat.)

Safe Harbor Seafood Restaurant

2510 2nd Ave N, Jacksonville Beach, FL 32250

(904) 479-3474

https://www.safeharborseafoodrestaurant.com/

Why we like it: Excellent fresh seafood served in a casual setting at a beautiful location near the intracoastal waterway. You order at the counter, and they serve you. Their main restaurant and market are in Mayport, but we love this one.

What we enjoy here: Mom loved the fried shrimp, and I was thrilled with the fresh catch and greens.

Mom says: I like this place and think it's a cheerful environment.

(We enjoyed a lunch with our awesome friends Ed Wilson and Beth Mihaly before they headed to California at this excellent seafood spot in Jax Beach.)

Sierra Grille

331 Marsh Landing Pkwy, Jacksonville Beach, FL 32250

(904) 273-2090   http://www.sierragrillesouth.com/

Why we like it: A favorite spot from the mid 90s, this casual counter service place has great southwestern healthy and delicious everything.

What we enjoy here: We love the soft tacos made with shrimp, chicken, beef, and fish. All grilled, light, and flavorful. Their salsa and condiment bar is rad. Fresh pineapple and the creamy dip are so good. So are the roasted red pepper and the verde.

Mom says: This is so simple, nice, and fun for an easy-going meal.

Sliders Oyster Bar

218 1st St, Neptune Beach, FL 32266

(904) 246-0881   https://www.slidersoysterbar.com/

Why we like it: Sliders is a consistent, good, casual seafood spot that has been around for decades.

What we like: Fish Tacos, Fresh Catch, Oysters. All excellent.

Mom says: Really comfortable environment and great food!

Ponte Vedra Beach

This beach community has grown exponentially and has some great new local spots that are casual and delicious.

Trasca and Co.

155 Tourside Drive, Suite 1500, Ponte Vedra Beach, FL 32082

(904) 395-3989   http://www.trascaandco.com/

Why we like it: Fun bright and casual coffee house and cafe.

What we enjoy here: Paninos (from a family recipe) make an outstanding and hearty breakfast, lunch, or dinner. Craft sodas, excellent baked goods, and coffee make this place a worthy Sawgrass Village destination.

Mom says: Wow this is good! I enjoyed the people here too.

(Mom, Mary Daley, me, and Sara Trasca)

Memphis Jax BBQ

10870 US-1, Ponte Vedra Beach, FL 32081

(904) 342-0078   http://www.memphisjaxbbq.com/

Why we like it: Casual spot in a great location between Jacksonville and St. Augustine and near Palm Valley. You order at the counter and they serve you.

What we like here: We shared an assorted platter of meats that were all perfect, served with outstanding sides. The greens, fried okra and macaroni and cheese were far above average, as was their homemade banana pudding.

Mom said, I'm glad we found out about this place and want to come back soon for more of this macaroni!

Palm Valley

Not so rustic anymore. But still beautiful and some great places.

Barbara Jean's

15 S Roscoe Blvd, Ponte Vedra Beach, FL 32082

(904) 280-7522   http://www.barbarajeans.com/

(The view from Barbara Jeans in Palm Valley)

Why we like it: A wonderful seafood and southern cooking restaurant that still feels like old Palm Valley. Beautiful setting on the Intracoastal Waterway and old timey décor.

What we enjoy here: Great crab cakes, bread basket, vegetables, and chocolate stuff for dessert.

Mom says: This is a country place, and I like it!

Palm Valley Outdoors Bar & Grill

377 S Roscoe Blvd, Ponte Vedra Beach, FL 32082

(904) 834-7183

https://palm-valley-outdoors-bar-grill.business.site/

Why we like it: Incredible old Florida setting, great food and people, and you've got to meet Roo!

What we enjoy here: We loved the view, people, and sitting outside. The fish spread was outstanding. Mom had a nice shrimp and grits and I had a fish special. All very good. Generous servings too.

Mom says: I think I just saw something walking around." I said, "Oh, that's Roo." Mom replied, "Mercy!"

Valley Smoke Restaurant

11 S Roscoe Blvd, Ponte Vedra Beach, FL 32082

(904) 285-3235   https://www.valleysmoke.com/

Why we like it: A recent first-class addition to Roscoe Road in Palm Valley, this waterfront restaurant feels like an incredible lodge in North Carolina. Incredible bar, indoor and outdoor dining.

What we enjoy here: Fantastic fried chicken, corn bread, pimento and cheese, steaks, Barbecue, burgers, seafood. Decadent desserts. Deviled eggs were delicious. Everything is high level and in a friendly environment.

Mom says: Rhis cornbread is too good. Everything is great.

(One of our closest friends, Beth Mihaly, recently took us to Valley Smoke when she was visiting from California. We are blessed with our friends and to be fortunate enough to enjoy such good food and beautiful settings!)

Nocatee

This newer town, just west of Ponte Vedra and Palm Valley, and East of U.S. 1/Phillips Highway, is bustling community that is beautiful to drive though and visit.

Traylor Park

158 Marketside, Ponte Vedra Beach, FL 32081

(904) 834-7356   https://www.treylorpark.com/nocatee

Why we like it: It's a little bit of Savannah in the First Coast. Excellent southern food and friendly service in a cool setting.

What we enjoy here: We absolutely loved the Avocado "Fries," I was crazy about the Low Country Boil. Mom was wild about their take on Chicken Pot Pie, which is wrapped in a flour tortilla, deep fried, and topped w/ fresh *pico de gallo*.

Mom says: A lot of food and a lot of flavor. Excellent!

Fruit Cove / Bayard

What used to be the middle of nowhere is now its own town.
Great places here too.

Lemongrass Thai Bistro

14866, Old St Augustine Rd, Suite 116 Jacksonville, FL
32258

(904) 647-5043 http://lemongrassjacksonville.com/

Why we like it: Beautiful and spacious Thai restaurant with
wonderful service and good food.

What we enjoy here: Mom loved the duck and I had a steak.
We were both very happy.

Mom says: I love how open it is, and it's just a fun place to
be.

The Pig Bar-B-Que

14985 Old St Augustine Rd #108, Jacksonville, FL 32258

(904) 374-0393   https://www.thepigbarbq.com/

Why we like it: A Jacksonville classic, there are a number of these around town, and they are great for a casual lunch or dinner.

(Banana Pudding after BBQ just seems right.)

What we enjoy here: I love the Baby Back Ribs and Mom loves the Pork Sandwich. The Banana Pudding is classic and good too.

Mom says: I always enjoy pigging out at The Pig!

Amaretti Desserts

14965 Old St Augustine Rd, Jacksonville, FL 32258

(904) 619-8279 http://www.amarettidesserts.com/index.html

Why we like it: This is a truly fantastic Bakery where you can enjoy a treat and a cup of Brass Tacks Coffee. They also just opened up an outpost in the San Marco Movie Theater.

What we enjoy here: Mom is wild about their Chocolate Cake and I think their Coconut Merengue is one of the best I've ever had.

Mom says: Just give me mine in a box so it will be easier to take it home. I know I can't eat all they give here, and I don't want to waste a bite!

(Incredible Chocolate Cake at Amaretti. Mom was happy!)

Vilano Beach

A visit to Vilano is one of our favorites, as it is so charming and low key there.

Aunt Kates

612 Euclid Ave, St Augustine, FL 32084

(904) 829-1105   https://aunt-kates.com/

Why we like it: Wonderful southern and old Florida waterfront restaurant.

What we enjoy here: Mom had the fried shrimp platter and I had the Maji Tacos. We were both thrilled and just loved being here.

Mom says: Don't skip the bread baskets. The cornbread is so old timey and delicious.

Beaches at Vilano

254 Vilano Rd, St Augustine, FL 32084

(904) 829-0589   http://www.beachesatvilano.com/menu/

Why we like it: The view is incredible of the fishing pier in Vilano and the food and service are very good. Love the super casual vibe and stepping back in time in a good way in this quaint town.

What we enjoy here: Blackened Fish Tacos, Fried Shrimp. My friend Jen loves their Mahi Sandwich.

Mom says: This feels like we're on a vacation.

Cap's On The Water

4325 Myrtle St, St Augustine, FL 32084

(904) 824-8794   http://www.capsonthewater.com/

Why we like it: One of our biggest pleasant surprises and best experiences was returning to this favorite place that has been significantly redone and revamped since recent hurricanes. What I remembered as a more rustic fish camp is now more of a fine dining resort on the water.

What we enjoy here: We shared a Crab appetizer that was beyond incredible, mom had a peanut crusted mahi special, and I had seared scallops. All was better than even hoped, and the bit of dessert was worth it too.

Mom says: I really feel like I've gone away on a nice vacation here.

Casa Benedetto's

2979, 165 Vilano Rd, St Augustine, FL 32084

(904) 471-5999   http://www.casabenedettos.com/

Why we like it: A charming little Italian restaurant with eclectic décor serving wonderful cuisine.

What we enjoy here: Excellent bread, salads, mom had pasta, and I had incredible chicken cacciatore.

Mom says: Remember this place. I want to come here again.

The Reef

4100 Coastal Hwy, St Augustine, FL 32084

(904) 824-8008   http://www.thereefstaugustine.com/

Why we like it: Beautiful Oceanfront dining with classic American cuisine.

What we enjoy here: Fried manchiego cheese bites with raspberry sauce, salmon, crab cakes and crème Brule.

Mom says: Such a nice place on the ocean.

St. Augustine

The oldest city in the United States with some of the best restaurants you'll find anywhere. We LOVE St. Augustine!

Amici Italian Restaurant

1915 A1A S, St Augustine Beach, FL 32080

(904) 461-0102   https://amicistaugustine.com/

(Thumbs up for excellent Lobster Ravioli at Amici!)

Why we like it: Outstanding family style Italian comfort food.

What we enjoy here: The shrimp appetizer was fantastic, as was the bread. Mom's pasta was a big hit, and I loved the fresh catch. Cannoli for dessert was perfection.

Mom says: Lots of good food!

A1A Aleworks Restaurant & Tap Room

1 King St, St Augustine, FL 32084

(904) 829-2977   http://www.a1aaleworks.com/

Why we like it: Great seafood place with an incredible view of the Bridge of Lions.

What we enjoy here: Mom had Mahi, I had tuna, and we started with an artichoke crab dip. All were perfection.

Mom says: This is like being in New Orleans or somewhere really special. Great way to see St. Augustine.

A1A Burrito Works: Taco Shop

671 A1A Beach Blvd, St Augustine, FL 32080

(904) 217-7451   http://www.burritoworks.com/

Why we like it: Amazing taco stand that will never let you down.

What we enjoy here: We got chicken and fish tacos and had so much fun eating them by the beach.

Mom says: This is the way to do things right here. A taco on the beach is really nice!

Athena Restaurant

4417, 14 Cathedral Pl, St Augustine, FL 32084

(904) 823-9076   https://athena-restaurant.business.site/

Why we like it: Excellent Greek food, traditional setting, nice service.

What we enjoy here: We shared an appetizer plate that was outstanding. I had lamb, mom had wonderful casseroles, and we shared the Baklava cheesecake. Incredible.

(Outstanding Baklava Cheesecake at Athena)

Mom says: This is enough for a whole family. Next time we're sharing. Let's come back soon.

Barnacle Bill's Seafood Restaurant

1302 N Ponce De Leon Blvd, St Augustine, FL 32084

(904) 494-2100

Why we like it: Recently relocated to the Holiday Inn, we were so happy to still have this St. Augustine Institution around—even with a more limited menu. It was Dad's favorite, and we always enjoy it.

What we enjoy here: Mom had fried shrimp and I had grilled Mahi. We were two happy people!

Mom says: I am so glad they are still around, but I miss the fish dip. It was my favorite.

Blue Hen Restaurant

117 M L King Ave, St Augustine, FL 32084

(904) 217-3777

Why we like it: My brother suggested we'd like this cute place in Lincolnville, and he was right. We really love it. It reminds me some of the old Blue Bird in Athens, Ga.

What we enjoy here: We started with Fried Green Tomatoes and Black-Eyed Pea Hummus, which were excellent. Mom had the Yard Bird plate, our friend Jen got the Fried Green Tomato BLT, and I tried the Datil Shrimp Tacos. We were all very pleased.

Mom says: What a treat to come to such a cute place and especially because we had our friend with us!

(We loved our visit to The Blue Hen Cafe in historic Lincolnville with our good friend and fellow Yoga Den instructor, Jennifer Delgado Sandifer.)

Borrillo's Pizzeria and Beer & Wine Garden

88 San Marco Ave, St Augustine, FL 32084

(904) 829-1133   https://www.borrillospizza.com/

Why we like it: Casual, fun, delicious, and nice people. Great patio dining too.

What we enjoy here: Big slices of pizza! Friendly service.

Mom says: A good piece of pizza makes a nice meal.

Brew |n| Dogz

1974 US-1, St Augustine, FL 32086

(904) 429-7149   https://brewz-n-dawgz.business.site/

Why we like it: Amazing hotdogs and cool craft beer place.

What we enjoy here: Dogs and onion rings.

(Mom said a hot dog for lunch sounded, "just right!" Brew |n| Dogz is an awesome local place. Great food and service!)

Mom says: Love this place. So good! Such nice people.

Brisky's BBQ

3009 N Ponce De Leon Blvd, St Augustine, FL 32084

(904) 907-2122   https://briskysbbq.business.site/

Why we like it: Such a nice southern and truly local-feeling barbeque restaurant with great lunch specials, homemade pies, and hospitable service. Plus it's located close to Fort Mose Historic State Park where we enjoy walking and enjoying the beautiful natural scenery of this area.

What we enjoy here: Mom loved the Baby Back Rib Sandwich, and I enjoyed the Brisket. The side dishes were great, and the Sweet Potato Pie a real treat.

Mom says: I've never seen such a big onion ring on a sandwich. This sure is good!

Chop Shop Artisan Butcher

600 Anastasia Blvd, St. Augustine, FL 32080

(904) 907-1312

Why we like it: This outstanding butcher shop, opened by Brian Whittington, chef and owner of the impressive **Preserved Restaurant** and **Smoked. Southern BBQ**, has created a fantastic fresh foods and gourmet market.

What we enjoy here: They have excellent cheese, charcuterie, and meats. We loved the Marcona Almonds, Pickled Okra, Berry Jam, and Oatmeal Cookies.

Mom says: I love things from here to add to a nice picnic lunch in the park.

Café Alcazar

25 Granada St, St. Augustine, FL 32084

(904) 825-9948   http://thealcazarcafe.com/cafe-alcazar/

Why we like it: This elegant, white-linen lunch spot located in the former pool area of the historic Hotel Alcazar, which was built by Henry Flagler in 1888. This beautiful property is now the Lightner Antique Museum, and it is not just old Florida; it's Old World. Excellent refined, classic cuisine, a beautiful setting, and excellent service make this a relaxing and enjoyable dining experience. I've loved it since the 80s and was happy to find things still outstanding when we visited recently. Reservations are highly recommended.

What we enjoy here: I love the Curried Chicken Salad and the Grilled Salmon topped with bechamel sauce and capers, served over Linguine. Mom likes their Shrimp Giovanni over Linguine. Their Tres Leches and Flourless Chocolate cakes are outstanding.

Mom says: Wow. This place is nice!

The Conch House

57 Comares Ave, St Augustine, FL 32080

(904) 829-8646   http://conch-house.com/

Why we like it: This is another beautiful resort spot to really get the Florida experience of sitting outside and seeing the Intra Coastal. It's a chill island vibe and a local's favorite eating and drinking spot for decades

What we enjoy here: The smoked fish spread was excellent. Mom had the friend shrimp plate and I had a large fresh fish special grilled. It was all basically perfect, as was our service.

Mom says: I really feel like I took a vacation coming here.

The Floridian

72 Spanish St, St Augustine, FL 32084

(904) 829-0655   http://www.thefloridianstaug.com/

Why we like it: An incredible eclectic spot that is one of our very favorites. We loved the old location and like this one even more. It's bigger with a designated bar area, and still nice outdoor seating and a good dining room too.

What we enjoy here: Awesome salads, innovative bowls, wonderful fresh catch, dessert case is out of this world. I love the pickled shrimp, mom loves the grits bowls, I had an awesome salad with fresh catch lately, and the Key Lime Pie was phenomenal.

(So much temptation at The Floridian.)

Mom says: This is definitely one of my favorites.

Jack's BBQ

691 A1A Beach Blvd, St Augustine, FL 32080

(904) 460-8100

Why we like it: Outstanding BBQ and sides that we picked up to go. It's a super casual bar feel with some outdoor seating areas too. You're super close to the beach. So, perfect for a picnic, which we had at Anastasia State Park because St. Augustine Beach was closed due to the hurricane approaching.

What we enjoy here: Mom had a pork sandwich with slaw and fries, and I had Baby Back Ribs with tater tots. Some of the best of both I've ever had.

Mom says: Let's do this again soon!

Culinary Outfitters

9 S Dixie Hwy # E, St Augustine, FL 32084

(904) 829-2727   http://culinaryoutfitters.org/

Why we like it: Beyond our hopes for a good lunch. Great people, place, open kitchen. We were really blown away. A new favorite for sure.

What we enjoy here: Everything. The best smoked salmon I've ever tasted. Great crab bits. Excellent deviled eggs. The desserts were terrific as was the lobster roll.

Mom says: This place is tops!

Burger Buckets and Fudge Buckets

3 Cordova St, St Augustine, FL 32084

(904) 342-5295   https://www.burgerbuckets.com/

Why we like it: A fun casual place for burgers on one side and an old fashioned ice cream parlor on the other. We are impressed by how friendly and helpful the servers are here on the restauarnt side and behind the counter in the ice cream parlor.

What we enjoy here: Mom likes the classic cheeseburger, and I am a fan of the Fudge Bacon Burger with Pepper Jack Cheese. The ice cream is good old Hersey's and a nice cool treat.

Mom says: I could get spoiled coming here! It's great and the people treat you very nicely.

Café Del Hidalgo

35 Hypolita St #101, St Augustine, FL 32084

(904) 823-1196

Why we like it: Paninis and Gelato in a charming setting

What we enjoy here: Mom had the apple and brie and I had one with Prosciutto and Pesto. They were both some of the best paninis we've ever tasted. Truly outstanding lunch.

(Café Del Hidalgo was fun and really good.)

Mom says: So crispy and delicious!

Carmillo's Pizzeria

146 W King St, St Augustine, FL 32084

(904) 494-6658   http://www.carmelosmarketplace.com/

Why we like it: Outstanding pizza in a casual environment. Excellent service and first-rate food.

What we enjoy here: We were so impressed with this place and have gone back a few times. Huge and amazing slices and excellent anti pasta salads here.

Mom says: Some of the best pizza I've ever had, and the people make it even better.

Catch 27

40 Charlotte St, St Augustine, FL 32084

(904) 217-3542   http://www.catchtwentyseven.com/

(Charming fresh seasonal seafood served here and prepared in creative ways. We loved sitting out back in the courtyard.)

Why we like it: Innovative and delicious

What we enjoy here: Fish dip, fresh catches.

Mom says: Wonderful experience!

City Bistro Tea House & Coffee Company

1280 N Ponce De Leon Blvd, St Augustine, FL 32084

(904) 209-6810   http://www.citybistrofl.com/

Why we like it: Great spot for breakfast, lunch, and dessert with an impressive assortment of teas.

What we enjoy here: We really enjoy the Apple Pastry and Pound Cake. The are served warm with whipped cream and a strawberry, and they are incredibly tasty afternoon treats.

Mom says: This pound cake reminds me of one my mother used to make. It's homemade and delicious. So nice!

Claude's Chocolates

6 Granada St, St Augustine, FL 32084

(904) 808-8395   http://www.claudeschocolate.com/

Why we like it: Chocolate

What we enjoy here: Chocolate

Mom says: Chocolate

Cousteau's Waffle and Milkshake Bar

15 Hypolita St, St Augustine, FL 32084

(904) 342-5627   http://www.wafflemilk.com/

Why we like it: Cute small place with indoor and outdoor seating in the old part of town.

What we enjoy here: There are numerous types of waffles available. We tried the crème brulee one and the Nutella with strawberries and loved them both.

Mom says: Don't bring me here too much or I can't stay on my diet.

Crave Food Truck

134 Riberia St, St Augustine, FL 32080

(904) 293-6373   https://cravestaug.com/

Why we like it: We are always craving Crave! A favorite: people, view, delicious!

(Me patriotic and repping my school on Memorial Day. I also picked Crave for my birthday lunch.)

What we like: Island bowls with rice, veggies, avocado, pineapple, shrimp, chicken, Ahi Tuna or Tempeh and their AMAZING ginger sauces, and you can also do it as a salad. They have an assortment of excellent salads, wraps and bowls. You can't go wrong with anything. Wraps. Love the Lime Hibiscus Yerba and they make great smoothies. Too good for words and healthy.

Mom (pictured with Crave owner, Andres) says: It's like a fun picnic here!

(An incredibly healthy and delicious salad with ginger dressing at Crave)

Crème de la Cocoa

299 San Marco Ave, St Augustine, FL 32084

(904) 466-9499   http://cremedelacocoa.com/

Why we like it: Beautiful upscale boutique sweet shop with nice people and outstanding delectables.

What we enjoy here: The cookies, macarons, toasted coconut chocolate covered marshmallow, and chocolates. This is a first-class place.

Mom says: What an incredible place!

Dessert First Bistro

121 Yacht Club Dr, St Augustine, FL 32084

(904) 417-0468   https://www.dessertfirstbistro.com/

(Mom loves this place and the cakes at Dessert First.)

Why we like it: We like the name and the desserts, and in fact, have not made it past their desserts, which we used to get at the Chocolate Turtle across from Flagler a few years ago.

What we enjoy here: We love the decadent Chocolate Cake and the cookies. Everything is made fresh and is high quality. They also serve lunch, which we hope to save room for one day.

Mom says: This is a chocolate cake! All the cakes are good here.

Diane's Natural Market Cafe

841 S Ponce De Leon Blvd Unit #6, St Augustine, FL 32084

(904) 808-9978   http://www.dianesnaturalmarket.com/

Why we like it: It's a beautiful café in one of our favorite natural food markets, in one of our favorite cities.

What we enjoy here: Mom loves the chicken salad, and I like the avocado and cheese sandwich. The vegetable chips are wonderful, and they have nice smoothies and juices.

Mom says: Fresh and delicious! Such a cheerful place too.

DOS Coffee & Wine

300 San Marco Ave, St Augustine, FL 32084

(904) 342-2421   https://www.dosbar.com/

Why we like it: We love hanging out at DOS. It is a big comfortable space that has lots of tables and a few sofas. We kill time here between yoga classes or on the way to or from an appointment.

What we enjoy here: They have incredible cookies, pour over coffees, pastries and light bits. Mom is crazy about their snickerdoodle and salted chocolate chip cookies.

Mom says: I like relaxing here, doing my puzzle, and enjoying life. Why not have some fun—and a cookie too?!

Drake's Deli

138 San Marco Ave, St Augustine, FL 32084

(904) 814-3557   http://www.drakesdeli.com/

Why we like it: My student, Gail at Yoga Den World Golf Village, recommended this place for a good sandwich. She was right. This cute little place has a nice outdoor seating area and very limited space inside. It was starting to rain when we were there, so they packaged it to-go for us. Very nice people with some of the best sandwiches and cakes I've ever had. Impressive an enjoyable place for sure. We look forward to many more visits here.

What we enjoy here: Mom thoroughly enjoyed the BLT, and I had a delicious Muffuletta. We also we very happy with the slices of Apple Cinnamon and Pineapple Upside Down Cake tried.

Mom says: Excellent sandwich and cake. Nice place and people!

Fiction Donuts

1835 US Highway 1 S. #139, St Augustine, FL 32084

(904) 679-3081   https://www.fictiondonuts.com/

Why we like it: The donuts are so good and unique that it's hard to believe they are real in this really cute and comfortable library themed donut shop. It's light and open and fun to pick up a dozen or enjoy one with a cup of coffee or soda.

What we enjoy here: Mom loves the old-fashioned glazed yeast donut here, and my favorite so far is the lemon curd. But I keep looking at the burnt honey with Rosemary. Time will tell…

Mom says: my parents owned donut shops, and this makes me think about them and those nice times.

Flavors Eatery

125 King St, St Augustine, FL 32084

(904) 824-4221   http://www.flavorseateryflorida.com/

Why we like it: Hearty and delicious wraps

What we enjoy here: Big wraps. Hot crispy and delicious. We both got chicken curries. Outstanding.

Mom says: Wow!

Fresh Market Island

110 A Anastasia Boulevard, St Augustine, FL 32080

(904) 417-0550   https://www.freshmarketisland.com/

Why we like it: Owners, Donna and Pieter Nel have created an impressive international wine and food emporium with a seating area, wine tastings, and wide array of first-rate gourmet foods, including frozen entrees, salads, dips, cheese, charcuterie, grass-fed beef, lamb, fresh baked bread, pies, and desserts.

What we enjoy here: We made a picnic lunch of blue cheese, fish dip, olives, a baguette, wafer crackers, broccoli, salad, and almonds. We were duly impressed and quite happy we found this remarkable and friendly place.

Mom says: Remember to come back here soon. This is good!

Gas Full Service Restaurant

9 Anastasia Blvd, St Augustine, FL 32080

(904) 217-0326   https://gasrestaurant.com/

Why we like it: A cheerful and casual restaurant with outstanding burgers and sandwiches. Generous servings and good service.

What we enjoy here: Mom loved the Cuban Burger and I had an excellent Flank Steak served with Black Beans and Rice.

Mom says: Now that's a burger!

Gourmet Hut

17 Cuna St, St Augustine, FL 32084

(904) 824-7477

Why we like it: One of the most unique and wonderful places we went on this culinary journey through Florida's First Coast. The outdoor dining in the heart of the historic area of town reminded me of New Orleans.

What we enjoy here: Food was cooked to order, the chef waited on us and cooked our dinner, which was superb. Mom had the duck, I had the filet. I hope to go back her soon.

Mom says: "They do things right here and make you feel really special."

(Chef Jermaine was so nice to mom. He suggested that she'd enjoy the Sweet Potato Hash with the Duck instead of Corn, and he was right. She loved it!)

Green Papaya Thai & Sushi Cuisine

841 S Ponce De Leon Blvd #10, St Augustine, FL 32084

(904) 516-8888   http://www.greenpapayathaisushi.com/

(We had a blast visiting Green Papaya, and, of course, had to take a picture in front of this cool wall.)

Why we like it: This is an impressive new place in St. Augustine that is dramatically decorated, offering excellent Thai classics with superior service.

What we enjoy here: We loved the Crab Rangoon, Avocado Salad and Udon Noodles House Special.

Mom says: This is a beautiful restaurant, and the food is generous, steaming hot, and delicious.

Growers Alliance

Growers Alliance Café And Gift Shop

(904) 371-7869   https://growersalliance.com/

Why we like it: A wonderful addition to Anastasia Island, this coffee shop, café, and gift shop offers excellent organic fair-trade coffee, delicious cheesecakes, samosas, live music, brunch, lunch, and dinner.

What we enjoy here: Mom loved the chocolate cheesecake, and I enjoyed the snickers. The coffee was excellent. We look forward to coming back for a samosa soon.

Mom says: Excellent Cheesecake and a pretty place!

Gypsy Cab Co Restaurant

828 Anastasia Blvd, St Augustine, FL 32080

(904) 824-8244   http://www.gypsycab.com/

Why we like it: An Anastasia Island classic, this place is consistently good for brunch, lunch or dinner.

(Enjoying a wonderful Sunday dinner at Gypsy Cab Co. with our family: Peggy and Grady H. Williams, Jr.)

What we enjoy here: We like their chicken with potatoes, seafood. Everything is good.

Mom says: These mashed potatoes are so good!

Hazel's Hot Dogs

2400 N Ponce De Leon Blvd, St Augustine, FL 32084

(904) 824-8484

Why we like it: A fantastic hot dog stand with picnic tables that is worth the drive.

What we enjoy here: Mom had a classic slaw dog, I had a chili dog, and we both loved the hand cut French fries.

Mom says: I like this place!

Hyppo Café and Coffee Bar

5718, 1765 Tree Blvd #5, St Augustine, FL 32084

(904) 342-7816   http://www.thehyppo.com/

Why we like it: Delicious fruit bars and sandwiches here. They also have locations in downtown St. Augustine and Jacksonville. They are expanding and offer these treats in many stores, including Native Sun and Natural Life.

What we enjoy here: Worth the drive for a hot crispy pressed sandwich and a cool treat.

(Mom loves the Strawberry popsicle here!)

Mom says: Refreshing and delicious.

Ice Plant Bar

110 Riberia St, St Augustine, FL 32084

(904) 829-6553   http://iceplantbar.com/

Why we like it: Very cool bar and restaurant in Saint Augustine with a city feel. Craft cocktails and innovative fresh classics.

What we enjoy here: I've only had brunch here once with my friend, Liz, and it was one of the best in my life. Pastries, steak and eggs, decadent dessert. I'd go back any chance I have for another meal.

(Incredible Short Rib Hash at The Ice Plant.)

Mom says: Thank you for the to-go lunch, but when do I get to go to this place?

The Kookaburra

1835 US-1 #133

(904) 209-9391   https://thekookaburracoffee.com/

Why we like it: Wonderful Coffee House with sweet and savory treats, great coffees and teas, and enjoyable place to hang out.

What we enjoy here: The meat pies make a delicious lunch or breakfast, the pour over coffees (done a few different ways) are fantastic, and the cookies are big and delicious.

Mom says: This is too much, but it sure is good!

(A cup of Hot Chocolate and Snickerdoodle Cookie at The Kookaburra was just a perfect late afternoon treat.)

La Pentola

58 Charlotte St, St Augustine, FL 32084

(904) 824-3282   https://lapentolarestaurant.com/

Why we like it: Outstanding continental cuisine served in an intimate old-old world, European dining room and a charming outside courtyard area. Impressive service. A truly enjoyable experience.

What we enjoy here: The olives with fresh herbs were a nice start. Great salads. Mom had a fish prepared Oscar style, and I had an excellent Ribeye Au Poivre. The dessert trio was superb. We loved everything.

Mom says: This is a special place with friendly people who make you feel welcome.

Luna Café

525 SR16, #130, St Augustine, FL 32084

(904) 209-5094

Why we like it: Charming

What we enjoy here: Meat Pies and Dessert

Mom says: Lovely people and place.

(Our visit to Luna Café was fantastic, and the food was delicious, the environment was wonderful)

The Manatee Café

525 FL-16 #106, St Augustine, FL 32084

(904) 826-0210   http://www.manateecafe.com/

Why we like it: This place reminds me of so many old school vegetarian and health food stores and restaurants. With friendly service, generous servings of hearty and delicious food, and a major local vibe, we definitely recommend this place.

What we enjoy here: We shared blue corn chips with Hummus and Tabouli. Mom had a Chicken Salad on a Croissant, and I had Black Bean Tacos. We ate a lot and had to go boxes.

Mom says: I really like this place. It's comfortable and such generous servings.

Mayday Ice Cream

1835 U.S. 1 South, Suite 127, St Augustine, FL 32084

(904) 342-2593 https://www.maydayicecream.com/

Why we like it: Deluxe ice cream parlor with cool flavors like ice triple vanilla and session chocolate that are nice updates on classis we all love. A new one just opened on Hendricks Ave. in Jacksonville while I was finishing this book.

What we enjoy here: We like the classics here in a cone and always say yes to the free cookie and sprinkles.

Mom says: You've got to live a little!

Michael's Tasting Room

25 Cuna St, St Augustine, FL 32084

(904) 810-2400   http://www.michaelstastingroom.com/

Why we like it: Dinner at this Spanish style restaurant was a standout dining experience because of charming building and dining room, excellent food, and superior service and hospitality.

What we like here: The shrimp and chorizo appetizer was revolutionary and the salad refreshing, light and flavorful. Mom had the tender short rib, and I had the superb Marcona Almond Stuffed Idaho trout with asparagus, Basque piperade, and garlic herb butter. All were beyond expectations. A truly sensational culinary experience.

Mom says: Wow!

Milagro On 12 Latin Kitchen

12 Avenida Menendez, St Augustine, FL 32084

(904) 679-4034

Why we like it: This place is situated right across from the fort, and we enjoyed a table with a beautiful view of it and the water. The food was fantastic, the servers were very nice and attentive, and the environment was relaxed and comfortable.

What we enjoy here: We shared an appetizer of shredded pork on top of tostones and a mixed grill platter. The flan was terrific too.

Mom says: Everything was really delicious, and we met more nice people.

Mojo's Tacos

551 Anastasia Blvd, St Augustine, FL 32080

(904) 829-1665

Why we like it: We love picking up to go or eating in the comfortable dining room area or out back on the patio. The tacos are fresh and delicious. You can get a nice Yerba Mate and crispy chips too.

What we enjoy here: All the tacos you need and want! Great shrimp, fish, chicken, pork. All are excellent.

Mom says: Let's pick up a taco and go to the beach!

Nalu's Tropical Take Out

1020 Anastasia Blvd, St Augustine, FL 32080

(904) 501-9592

(Our good friend Liz Robbins and Mom. Thank you for introducing us to this great place, Liz!)

Why we like it: This place is so good and fun to visit too. Conveniently located at the entrance to Anastasia State Park. Our friend Liz introduced us to this, and we sure do appreciate it.

What we enjoy here: I loved the Ahi Burger, mom had a Chicken Sandwich, and Liz had a wrap. All of us were very happy and had fun sitting outside together.

Mom says: I love a picnic lunch and good friends make it even nicer! Wonderful!

Ned's Southside Kitchen

2450 US-1, St Augustine, FL 32086

(904) 794-2088   http://www.nedssouthside.com/

Why we like it: This casual American eatery has a wide array of excellent appetizers, salads, entrees, and desserts. The servings are generous, with reasonable prices and friendly service, and they even have a pick-up window you can drive through for to-go orders.

What we enjoy here: We were impressed with the coconut shrimp and pineapple salsa. Mom had a fantastic chicken entrée with fresh vegetables, and I had a New Orleans style seafood etouffee. The Strawberry cake was wonderful.

Mom says: I really like it here and hope to come back again soon. They give you a lot of tasty food!

O.C. White's Seafood & Spirits

118 Avenida Menendez, St Augustine, FL 32084

(904) 824-0808   http://www.ocwhitesrestaurant.com/

Why we like it: A charming restaurant in a historic building and courtyard located near the Bridge of Lions in St. Augustine.

What we enjoy here: We loved the hot artichoke and crab dip, mom had the best Shrimp and Grits she's had since we started this project, and I had an excellent pan seared fresh catch.

(Mom was thrilled with our visit to O.C. White's and loved the generous amount of bacon with the shrimp and grits...)

Mom says: I really feel like I'm on vacation here, and I have to be careful not to eat so much. This is too good!

One Twenty Three Burger House

123 King St, St Augustine, FL 32084

(904) 687-2790   http://onetwentythreeburgerhouse.com/

Why we like it: Excellent Burgers and Service in a great setting. Sitting on the porch was wonderful.

What we enjoy here: Mom had a classic cheeseburger and fries and I had a burger with no bun, an egg, and extra avocado.

Mom says: I love a good cheeseburger, and this is a good cheeseburger here.

(We had a great time sitting on the front porch here and appreciate our good friend, Geneva Polk telling us to come here.)

Osprey Tacos

300 Anastasia Blvd, St Augustine, FL 32080

(904) 679-4191   http://ospreytacos.com/

Why we like it: Our friend Liz Robbins came to my Mind Body class at Yoga Den World Golf Village and said this was the place for lunch that day. We sure are glad she did! Charming spot with outdoor picnic tables and excellent tacos.

What we enjoy here: Liz had vegan tacos, I had fish and steak, mom had fried chicken and pork belly. We were all very happy with our choices and enjoyed chips and salsa.

Mom says: Liz always picks good places! I liked sitting outside here.

Osteen's Restaurant

205 Anastasia Blvd, St Augustine, FL 32080

(904) 829-6974   http://www.osteensrestaurant.com/

Why we like it: This cash only old-fashioned institution has been around for decades because it is one of the best southern seafood and country cooking around. It is a favorite of many friends and family, and we always love going here.

What we enjoy here: You just can't beat their fried shrimp. They also have excellent Minorcan Clam Chowder, fried chicken, chicken livers, and pork chops, squash casserole, and pies.

Mom says: Such a cute place with good food. Nice to come early and try to beat the crowd.

Peace Pie

8 Aviles St, St Augustine, FL 32084

(904) 295-8232   https://www.peacepieworld.com/

Why we like it: Amazing cool place. Great concept and people! Insanely good ice cream sandwiches with a layer of pie in them.

What we enjoy here: I had the cookies and cream and mom had the strawberry shortcake

Mom says: I don't know how you found this place, but I'm glad you did!

(It's easy to feel peaceful on the patio at Peace Pie.)

Petit Pleasures Bakery

125 A1A Beach Blvd, St Augustine, FL 32080

(904) 679-3411

Why we like it: Charming French Bakery and Café that is authentic and quite unique to our area.

What we enjoy here: Mom went for Chicken and I had seafood, and both of these hot savory crepes were superb. The pastries are over the top delicious too. Outstanding experience and love picking up treats at the outpost on Cathedral Place downtown, near St. George Street.

Mom says: The crepes and desserts are outstanding!

Pizzalley's Chianti Room

60 Charlotte St, St Augustine, FL 32084

(904) 825-4100   https://pizzalleyschiantiroom.com/

Why we like it: They have some of the best pizza, bread, salads, and Italian fare around. It's a bustling place with a small pizza part, nice big dining room, and charming front porch. Good service and a fun time coming here.

What we enjoy here: I'm a huge fan of their Chicken Marsala, and mom loves the Piccata.

Mom says: This serving is enough to feed a family. Very good!

Present Moment Café

226 W King St, St Augustine, FL 32084

(904) 827-4499   http://www.presentmomentcafe.com/

Why we like it: Very different and good raw vegan café.

What we enjoy here: Everything. Salads. Tacos. Cashew Ice cream.

Mom says: I don't know how they made cashews into ice cream, but I like it.

Preserved Restaurant

102 Bridge St, St Augustine, FL 32084

(904) 679-4940   https://preservedrestaurant.com/

Why we like it: Old world, southern, and elegant. Reminds me of Charleston and Savanah.

What we enjoyed: We had Sunday Brunch and loved the Scones, Eggs Benedict with fried oysters, Apple Gallate with ice cream. We hope to go to dinner here soon. It was epic.

Mom says: It is real treat to have had brunch here on their front porch and enjoy the beautiful day.

The Press

525 FL-16 #101, St Augustine, FL 32084

(904) 217-8254   http://www.thepressstaugustine.com/

Why we like it: Great craft beer and wine bar vibe with deluxe food to go with it. Casual and nice all the way around. Many thanks to our friend Dianne from Yoga Den World Golf Village for telling us about it.

What we enjoy here: Mom had an incredible fried chicken sandwich, and I had a fish sandwich. We shared their award-winning white chocolate bread pudding, and it was insanely good.

Mom says: Remember this place. Make a note of it. I want to come back here!

Raintree

102 San Marco Ave, St Augustine, FL 32084

(904) 824-7211   http://raintreerestaurant.com/

Why we like it: This beautiful restaurant in an old Victorian home is casual and elegant place that has been a destination for decades. They serve fine traditional cuisine for brunch, lunch, and dinner.

What we enjoy here: I love their Escargot and Beef Wellington, and mom enjoys their Jumbo Shrimp and Lobster Pasta. They also have excellent desserts such as Chocolate Mouse and Crème Brulee.

Mom says: This big old house reminds me of growing up near Savannah and visiting my family there. Wonderful place!

(Me, mom, Grady H. Williams, Peggy Williams, and our good friend Paula Emery celebrating at Raintree)

Relámpago Coffee Lab

74 Spanish St, St Augustine, FL 32084

(904) 484-7241   https://www.relampagocoffee.com/

Why we like it: An excellent coffee house located in a charming old house with seating areas inside and on the front porch. They are owned by the same people as DOS, and have an impressive array of coffees, teas, baked goods, and oatmeal.

What we enjoy here: I love a pour over coffee, and mom is a fan of their cookies.

Mom says: It is fun sitting here on the front porch and watching people walk by.

Saltwater Cowboys

299 Dondanville Rd, St Augustine, FL 32080

(904) 471-2332   http://www.saltwatercowboys.com/

Why we like it: This is my kind of old Florida. Absolutely beautiful cracker style house on the marshes of the Intracoastal Waterway.

What we enjoy here: Shrimp Dondanville Appetizer is not to be missed and we shared a wonderful fried chicken dinner with all the fixings.

Mom says: Take me back here again soon.

Schooner's Seafood House

3560 N Ponce De Leon Blvd, St Augustine, FL 32084

(904) 826-0233   http://www.schooners-seafood.com/

Why we like it: Classic local favorite with traditional southern seafood and steaks. My friend Paula said we'd like it here, and she was right.

What we enjoy here: Mom had the fried shrimp and I had a broiled combination plate. We were quite impressed and look forward to returning soon.

Mom says: The fried shrimp are light, crispy, and delicious.

Smoked. Southern Barbeque

11 Magnolia Ave, St Augustine, FL 32084

(904) 824-8222   https://smokedsouthernbbq.com/

Why we like it: An inspired and incredible treasure on the grounds of the Fountain of Youth. Eating here stands out as a fun and delicious experience.

What we enjoy here: We went all out and loved it all

Mom says: This is the life!

Smokin D's BBQ

110 FL-206, St Augustine, FL 32086

(904) 797-2050   http://www.smokindbbq.com/

Why we like it: Some of the best barbeque we've ever tasted.

What we enjoy here: Mom likes the pork sandwich and I like the brisket. Great beans and slaw.

Mom says: Eating outside here and looking at the water is really fun.

Swillirbees Donuts

8 Granada St, St Augustine, FL 32084

(904) 217-8622   https://www.swillerbees.com/

(Liz, mom, and reflections of me at a great donut place!)

Why we like it: Absolutely incredible donut shop. Homemade craft goodies abound her.

What we enjoy here: We love the Phone Home Reece's Pieces, Apple Strudel, and Classic Glazed. Great Cinnamon Roll too!

Mom says: I always love a good donut, and this is a *really good* donut.

Tropicali Food Truck

606 N Ponce De Leon Blvd, St Augustine, FL 32084

(904) 466-4527

Why we like it: Really cute food truck with very nice people who once jumped started our car when I spaced out while we were pigging out and listening to Wilco on a beautiful fall day and drained the battery! They recently moved, and we don't care where they go, we're following them.

What we enjoy here: The Chicken Riblets! I don't know exactly what they are other than delicious. They are like Teriyaki pieces of heaven topped with some shredded coconut. The fresh mahi with beans, rice, and plantains is so amazing. Mom loves their pork plate too.

Mom says: Always bring a cooler when we come here. I don't want any of this to go to waste. So good!

2 Creeks Bar & Grill

74 Capulet Drive #201, St Augustine, FL 32092

(904) 217-3230

Why we like it: This neighborhood spot is just around the corner from where I teach at Yoga Den World Golf Village, and it's a beautiful place with good food and service.

What we enjoy here: Steamed Shrimp, Pork Rinds, Tomato Bisque, Open Faced Roast Beef Sandwich, Burgers, and Tacos.

Mom (pictured with me and our friend Geeta) says: I really enjoy a hot open-faced sandwich—especially on a colder day. I'm always happy with a burger here too.

Uptown Scratch Kitchen

300 San Marco Ave, St Augustine, FL 32084

(904) 377-6050

Why we like it: A top-notch food truck located adjacent to DOS Coffeehouse where you can eat in the outdoor picnic area or in DOS. They cook the food to order, and they serve you. Friendly and fresh. This is a winner.

What we enjoy here: Shrimp Po Boy, Fish and Grits, Fried Chicken, Hamburgers, French Fries with Garlic and Rosemary.

Mom says: This takes some time while they cook your food fresh for you, the servings are huge, and it is fantastic.

Woodpecker's Backyard BBQ

4930 FL-16A, St Augustine, FL 32092

(904) 531-5670   https://woodpeckersbbq.weebly.com/

Why we like it: A rustic and charming spot in the Orangedale area with delicious barbeque, side dishes, and desserts in a beautiful part of town. They close when they run out each day. So, come early!

What we enjoy here: Great ribs, sausage, pork, brisket, and turkey. The Datil pepper corn and baked beans are spicy and so delicious. Excellent Hummingbird Cake.

Mom says: I love sitting at these picnic tables and eating this good barbeque feast any time.

Mayport

This little village was a family favorite during my childhood that we still love to visit today.

Sandollar Restaurant

9716 Heckscher Dr, Jacksonville, FL 32226

(904) 251-2449   http://sandollarrestaurantjax.com/

Why we like it: Right across the river with a view of Mayport, this casual seafood restaurant is a treasure.

What we enjoy here: Amazing BBQ Shrimp, Onion Rings, Fresh Catch Specials, and the best Sweet Potato Fries ever with very good service.

Mom says: This view is really enjoyable, and the food is delicious. I like riding on the Mayport Ferry to come here!

Simply Tasty Thai

2292 Mayport Rd # 8, Atlantic Beach, FL 32233

(904) 372-2600   https://www.simplytastythai.com/

Why we like it: Outstanding Thai

What we enjoy here: Appetizer Sampler and Noodle dishes

Mom says: Excellent!

(We were really thrilled with our dinner at Simply Tasty Thai.)

Singleton's Seafood Shack

4728 Ocean St, Atlantic Beach, FL 32233

(904) 246-4442

Why we like it: Classic Fish Camp. This is one of my all-time favorite places for the Florida vibe, the excellent food, the good service, and the whole experience. It's a fun place where we've met friends and family for ages.

What we enjoy here: Fish Dip and Fried Shrimp. Low Country Boil. It's all good and fresh here.

Mom says: Wonderful!

(Pure bliss at Singleton's Seafood Shack!)

(My godson, Nathan Reeder, Me, Mom, good friend, Wanda
Jacobs, and my goddaughter, Charlotte Reeder enjoying
Sunday lunch at Singletons.)

Amelia Island / Fernandina Beach

A visit up to this beautiful island and historic beach and downtown is always a wonderful experience. Southern and truly charming in a relaxed, non-pretentious way. This is Old Florida at its best.

Brett's Waterway Café

1 S Front St, Fernandina Beach, FL 32034

(904) 261-2660

https://www.ameliaisland.com/Dining/Bretts-Waterway-Cafe

Why we like it: Our visit to Brett's was a highlight of this project because of the incredible waterfront view we enjoyed sitting outside, the superior service, and truly amazing fresh seafood specials. This felt like vacation and relaxing and so enjoyable on all levels.

What we enjoyed here: Mom had the Cobia Oscar and I had the Swordfish special. We were truly impressed. Generous servings and very flavorful. Outstanding preparation on both.

Mom says: This is some of the best fish I've ever tasted, and I love these mashed potatoes.

The Cinnamon Bear Country Store

107 Centre St, Fernandina Beach, FL 32034

(904) 432-7932   https://cinnamonbearstores.com/

Why we like it: This is a really cute gift store with lots of gourmet goodies, candies, and ice cream.

What we enjoy here: Finding jars of peppers, mustard, preserves, and relishes and other treats. Great ice cream and candies too.

Mom says: This is a fun place to get a snack for the ride home. I like the VW bug. It reminds me of the ones I used to drive.

Gilbert's Underground Kitchen

510 S 8th St, Fernandina Beach, FL 32034

(904) 310-6374 http://www.undergroundkitchen.co/

(Lunch was served from the kitchen counter in to-go containers, and they let you eat in, picnic style. We got a half Fried Chicken with Biscuits, Macaroni and Cheese, Collard Greens, Potato Salad, and Crispy Brussels Sprouts. Mom said, this is delicious--so tasty and a great variety! She wasn't kidding.)

Why We like it: Southern comfort!

What we enjoy here: Fried chicken and BBQ. Peach and Pecan Pies

Mom says: This is some good country cooking!

Fantastic Fudge

218 Centre St, Fernandina Beach, FL 32034

(904) 277-4801   http://www.fantasticfudge.com/

Why we like it: This is a picture-perfect, old-fashioned candy store and ice cream parlor. Large marble-top tables to make the fudge are on display, as are outstanding fudge, candies, and other homemade confections. The ice cream is fantastic too.

What we enjoy here: Their Rocky Road fudge is some of the best ever, and a nice ice cream cone is always a nice treat.

Mom says: There goes my diet! But this is worth it.

Nana Teresa's Bake Shop

13 N 3rd St, Fernandina Beach, FL 32034

(904) 277-7977 http://nanateresa.com/

Why we like it: A charming old-fashioned bakery in historic Downtown Fernandina Beach, this is a great place to pick up excellent sweets or slow down and enjoy something in this quant setting.

What we enjoy here: We had an almond cream and fresh fruit pastry, and they were decadent and delicious. There's a great assortment of macarons, cookies, and cupcakes too. Mom had an Italian soda, and I had an Americana coffee. Wonderful!

Mom says: I like this place; the pastries are delicious. I even like your hat, but I'd like it better if you weren't wearing it at the table.

Sliders Seaside Grill

1998 S Fletcher Ave, Fernandina Beach, FL 32034

(904) 277-6652   https://www.slidersseaside.com/

Why we like it: A fun ocean front restaurant with indoor and outdoor dining at Fernandina Beach with excellent food and gracious service. We loved sitting out back overlooking the ocean and taking in the large crowd and live entertainment on a beautiful summer afternoon.

What we enjoy here: We shared the Homemade Baked Lobster and Crab Dip, which was hearty, creamy, and delicious with the crispy tortilla chips.

Mom says: Good food, friendly people, and a view of the beach make this place a real special time.

T-Rays Burger Station

202 S 8th St, Fernandina Beach, FL 32034

(904) 261-6310   http://www.traysburgerstation.com/

Why we like it: Super cool and casual lunch spot with a nice Southern vibe in an old gas station on the main drag in Fernandina. Excellent food and service. You can sit outside or inside for a fun time with friendly service.

What we enjoy here: They have the reputation of having some of the best hamburgers in the country and the best fried shrimp on the Island. We tried both and were really pleased.

Mom says: I don't know how you found out about this place, but I'm sure glad you did.

Crescent Beach

This charming beach community, just south of St. Augustine Beach, is worth the drive for us every time we get to go, whish is not often enough.

South Beach Grill

45 Cubbedge Rd, St Augustine, FL 32080

(904) 471-8700   http://www.southbeachgrill.net/

Why we like it: Amazing ocean view, very relaxed, excellent food. Our outstanding server made us feel comfortable too.

What we enjoy here: We loved the crab cakes, mom had a fresh catch and grits, I had it Mediterranean style. We were very happy and enjoyed a piece of classic Key lime pie.

Mom says: I can't believe this view of the beach and such good food.

Viola's Pizza

6149 A1A S, St Augustine, FL 32080

(904) 471-2981

Why we like it: Great Italian restaurant and pizzeria down in charming Crescent beach with excellent food and friendly service.

What we enjoy here: We LOVED the pizza!

Mom says: Now this is really good. You can't beat hot crispy pizza.

High Springs

A drive down to High Springs, through Alachua, and to Gainesville, then on to Micanopy is a wonderful thing.

Great Outdoors Restaurant

65 N Main St, High Springs, FL 32643

(386) 454-1288   https://greatoutdoorsrestaurant.com/

Why we like it: This place is worth the drive to High Springs, which in itself is pretty charming Old Florida.

What we enjoy here: I love the Scallop salad, Mom loves the chicken Salad Sandwich. Everything is beyond what you'd hope for. I had an excellent Prime Rib here too.

Mom says: I hope I can have a to go box and that you have a cooler in the car.

Alachua

Conestogas Restaurant

14920 N Main St, Alachua, FL 32615

(386) 462-1294   http://www.conestogasrestaurant.com/

Why we like it: Charming traditional family restaurant. Nice people in charming downtown Alachua. Thank you to my friend Will Croft from West Jax Rotary for suggesting it!

What we enjoy here: Mom loved the burger. I enjoyed a ribeye baked potato and salad with blue cheese dressing. Excellent classics. You pay on the way out in the ice cream and candy shop she they have a nice selection of Blue Bell.

Mom says: I'd like to come here any time we can to enjoy the beautiful drive and small-town area.

Gainesville

Ballyhoo

3700 W University Ave, Gainesville, FL 32607

(352) 373-0059   http://www.ballyhoogrill.com/

What why we like it: Great casual Florida style grill with excellent seafood, steaks, burgers, oysters, salads. Consistent and a nice laid-back place not far from UF campus. I've loved this place since the early 2000s.

What we enjoy here: Mom loves the Cuban sandwich here and cheeseburger. The salads with ham, fresh grouper, filet, and cedar plank salmon are some of the standout dishes.

Mom says: Too much good food. These servings are huge!

Dorn's Liquors and Wine Warehouse

4140 NW 16th Blvd, Gainesville, FL 32605

352) 378-0229

Why we like it: a gourmet treasure.

What we enjoy here: the cheese corner is superb. Excellent Serrano Ham, Prosciutto, Salami. Olives, cornichons, mustard, and truffle mousse and country pates. Lots of International and domestic cheeses.

Mom says: I like everything and especially the chocolate toffee almonds.

Gigi's Cupcakes

3524 SW Archer Rd #130, Gainesville, FL 32608

(352) 240-6122

https://gigiscupcakesusa.com/pages/gainesville-florida

Why we like it: An outstanding cupcake shop that we've enjoyed for over a decade. They have great classic and gluten free options.

What we enjoy here: They are all really good. We especially enjoy the Red Velvet and Carrot Cake.

Mom says: I like their chocolate and yellow cake a lot too.

Emiliano's Cafe

7 SE 1st Ave, Gainesville, FL 32601

(352) 375-7381 http://emilianoscafe.com/

Why we like it: A favorite place for us since the 80s. Nice indoor and outdoor seating in charming downtown Gainesville.

What we enjoy here: The tostones with aioli, chicken and yellow rice, garlic shrimp, steak. All outstanding. Wonderful flan and other seasonal desserts.

Mom says: This reminds me of Ybor city. So nice!

(Living large at Emiliano's!)

Maude's Coffee

101 SE 2nd Pl, Gainesville, FL 32601

(352) 336-9646

Why we like it: Cool college town indie coffee house.

What we enjoy here: Coffee and chocolate cake. Their desserts are always enjoyable.

Mom says: Chocolate cake is always good for me.

(Sharing good cake and conversation at Maude's with our wonderful friend, Jody Hedge.)

Mildred's Big City Food

3445 W University Ave, Gainesville, FL 32607

(352) 371-1711   http://mildredsbigcityfood.com/

Why we like it: Classic Gainesville eatery with counter service lunch and white-linen service for dinner

What we enjoy here: Everything is first rate. Excellent salads and soups. Mom loves the quiche. I enjoy the sloppy joe and ham and brie sandwich. Coconut, chocolate, carrot and other seasonal cakes are stellar.

Mom says: what a wonderful place to spend time with a friend or family.

(With a favorite friend, Jody Hedge at a favorite place, Mildred's!)

New Deal Café

3443 W University Ave, Gainesville, FL 32607

(352) 371-4418

Why we like it: A casual neighbor and counterpart to Mildred's Big City, this is a great spot for lunch or dinner with some nice outdoor seating.

What we enjoy here: We love the toasts, burgers, and I love being able to order the fresh catch off the Mildred's menu here too. Great wines, coffee, tea and desserts.

Mom says: This is my kind of place!

Phenomenon Nitrogen Ice Cream & Bake Shop

3524 SW Archer Rd #140, Gainesville, FL 32608

(754) 216-3478   http://www.phenomenom320.com/

Why we like it: innovative, cool, friendly, and incredible ice cream made to order with liquid nitrogen.

What we enjoy here: mom had strawberry and I had cookies and cream. We shared a decadent smores cookie. All insanely good.

Mom says: This is great ice cream!

Public and General Restaurant

1000 NE 16th Ave, Gainesville, FL 32601

(352) 745-7358   http://publicandgeneral.com/

Why we like it: Real neat old general store and local bar feel.

What we enjoy here: Incredibly delicious sandwiches and the dilled French fries with creamy tomato dip were off the charts.

Mom says: Those fries are outstanding!

Southern Charm Kitchen

1714 SE Hawthorne Rd, Gainesville, FL 32641

(352) 505-5553   http://www.southerncharmkitchen.com/

Why we like it: cute small place with excellent southern soul food.

(This roast chicken with caramel sauce at Southern Charm Kitchen is insanely good.)

What we enjoy here: mom loves the chicken and waffle. I love the roast chicken.

Mom says: This is newer to me having this together, and I really enjoy it.

Uppercrust Bakery

3506, 4116 NW 16th Blvd, Gainesville, FL 32605

(352) 376-7187   http://uppercrustgnv.com/

Why we like it: Like a religious experience and one of the best bakeries I've ever been to anywhere.

What we enjoy here: Wonderful baguettes and Batard Bread. They have a nice assortment of pates, cheeses, excellent iced cookies. Nice fresh fruit and truly impressive pastries are available here. Great Jams and Lemon Curd.

Mom says: This place is nice. Let's sit outside here and enjoy something good before we hit the road.

Micanopy

Old Florida Café

203 NE Cholokka Blvd, Micanopy, FL 32667

(352) 466-3663

Why we like it: Old school lunch counter vibe that's like a charming historic piece of Marjorie Rawlins old Florida. We love sitting outside here on a nice day.

What we enjoy here: Quaint lunch spot that's worth a drive for the Cuban Sandwich and the Black beans and rice.

Mom says: I like this a lot!